Donald Davidson's Philosophy of Language

DONALD DAVIDSON'S PHILOSOPHY OF LANGUAGE

An Introduction

BJØRN T. RAMBERG

Basil Blackwell

First published 1989

Basil Blackwell Ltd
108 Cowley Road, Oxford, OX4 1JF, UK

Basil Blackwell Inc.
432 Park Avenue South, Suite 1503
New York, NY 10016, USA

British Library Cataloguing in Publication Data

A CIP catalogue record for this book is available from the British Library.

Library of Congress Cataloging in Publication Data

Ramberg, Bjørn T.
  Donald Davidson's philosophy of language: an introduction/Bjørn
T. Ramberg.
    p.   cm.
  Bibliography: p.
  Includes index.
  ISBN 0-631-16458-8. − ISBN 0-631-16786-2 (pbk.)
  1. Davidson, Donald, 1917- − Contributions in philosophy of
language. 2. Languages − Philosophy. I. Title.
P85.D38R35 1989   88-34864
121'.68 − dc19   CIP

Typeset in 11 on 13 pt Garamond
by Setrite Typesetter, Hong Kong
Printed in Great Britain by
T.J. Press (Padstow) Ltd, Padstow, Cornwall.

Contents

Acknowledgements

For their inspiration, philosophical and other, I would like to thank my good friends in and around the Department of Philosophy of Queen's University, Kingston. That is where I learned much of what I know about philosophy, and that is where the bulk of this book was written. In particular, it is a pleasure to acknowledge Carlos Prado, whose generous support throughout the project has been invaluable. Naturally, no one but the author is to blame for the errors and misapprehensions that remain.

Parts of chapters 6 and 8 draw on my paper 'Charity and Ideology: The Field Linguist as Social Critic', scheduled to appear in *Dialogue*. I thank the editor for permission to use this material.

Finally, no one deserves thanks more than Michael, who was there every step of the way. This book is for her.

BTR
Oslo, August 1988

1
Introduction

There is no such thing as a language. This is the remarkable conclusion of Donald Davidson's recent paper, 'A Nice Derangement of Epitaphs' (Davidson, 1986a). What are we to make of this claim? Davidson made his formidable reputation as a philosopher in large measure through a series of ground-breaking studies in semantics published over the last three decades.[1] Is he now calling into question the very existence of what these papers purport to be about?

Such a sweeping recantation is not what Davidson intends. He is not looking to deprive the study of language of its subject matter. He is, rather, urging that we revise some commonly held ideas about how linguistic communication works. What his arguments lead him to conclude, is that

> there is no such thing as a language, not if a language is anything like what many philosophers and linguists have supposed. There is therefore no such thing to be learned, mastered, or born with. We must give up the idea of a clearly defined shared structure which language-users acquire and then apply to cases. (Davidson, 1986a, p. 446).

Davidson is not giving up his search for a description of the nature of linguistic competence, the elusive goal of his philosophical efforts over the last 25 years. He is suggesting that the concept of a language is an obfuscatory hindrance to that task. This claim amounts to more than a slightly hyperbolic dismissal from service of a conceptual tool. Davidson is making a philosophically substantive point, and his target is a powerful and highly plausible idea. For what could linguistic competence be, if not the mastery of a clearly defined shared structure, the mastery of an integrated, unitary system that speaker and interpreter have in common?

The considerations that have led Davidson to reject this seemingly persuasive explanatory strategy surface explicity in 'Communication and Convention' (*Inquiries*, pp. 265–80). This paper, first published in 1983, is by three years the most recent of the ones collected in *Inquiries into Truth and Interpretation*. Its ammunition is directed at various attempts to explain linguistic communication in terms of conformity to a body of conventions. It is easy to see how closely related this topic is to Davidson's later attack on the concept of a language. In so far as we think of a language as a clearly defined shared structure, we must conceive of any particular language as constituted by a particular social practice. And a social practice is specifiable in terms of the conventions that govern it. But what Davidson attempted to show in 1983, was that 'convention does not help explain what is basic to linguistic communication' (*Inquiries*, p. 280). If linguistic communication does not essentially involve conventions, in what sense is it a specifiable practice? And if it is not a specifiable social practice, what content can we give to the notion of a language? None, is Davidson's recent conclusion.

Not surprisingly, this dramatic pronouncement has met with resistance, notably from Ian Hacking (1986) and Michael Dummett (1986). They argue that Davidson's conclusion is unwarranted. Hacking, in particular, thinks that in drawing it Davidson is *ipso facto* retracting some of the central premises of his earlier papers. On the reading of Davidson that I develop below, Hacking and Dummett are wrong on both counts.

The guiding intuition behind my interpretation of Davidson is that all his writings on language can be read as attempts to exorcise the ghosts of reification from out thinking about communication. On this view, Davidson's challenge to the very idea of a language emerges as a natural development of his theory of meaning.

In papers published in the 1960s and 1970s, Davidson carefully develops a philosophy of language purified of the reification of meaning and reference. More recently, he has focused on the reification involved in the notion of a language itself. It turns out that the concept of a language, like the notion of meanings of words and the idea of a relation of reference, can do no work in an account of linguistic competence. All three are conceptual parasites, gaining any content they might have only as the theoretical constructs of a model of linguistic communication that derives its explanatory power from another source: the concept of truth.

It is true that in developing his comprehensive philosophy of language Davidson does write as if we can make good sense of the concept of a language. But this does not imply that the validity of his theory hinges on this assumption, unless we imagine the progression of philosophical thought to be a matter of deductive construction. Like the boards in Otto Neurath's ship, the concepts of a language, of meaning and of reference cannot be replaced all at once. By taking for granted that there are languages, Davidson was able to articulate a theory of meaning which in turn enabled him to subject this very natural supposition itself to critical scrutiny. The result, I hope to show, is not a theory which undercuts itself, but a comprehensive, coherent account of the phenomenon of linguistic communication.

My reconstruction of Davidson's empirical, holistic and dynamic picture of language is intended ultimately as a semantic underpinning for a holistic understanding of critical rationality. While I believe the account is Davidsonian in spirit and in all its fundamental features, I cannot claim that it is in every detail a faithful representation or development of Davidson's own current theory. Of the arguments developed in the chapters ahead, those that are not explicitly made by Davidson are certainly inspired by his thinking. But this is not to say that he would give them all his stamp of approval. Nor is that stamp required. My project is not primarily one of exegesis; it does not matter all that much how Davidson's thought actually developed over the course of writing the papers I draw on. The dialectic I am after is conceptual, not chronological. Nor is it important that he be pinned down in cases where textual evidence reveals some vacillation. I am not concerned to make a contribution to the history of ideas. In the present context, getting Davidson right is not an end in itself, but a means, an extremely valuable means, to getting language right.

In chapter two, I draw the contrast between semantics and

epistemology, sorting out some ambiguities that threaten our understanding of the idea of a theory of truth. First I give a general explication of the questions Davidson takes himself to be answering. This is followed by a brief account of a few key features of Davidson's primary source of inspiration, the philosophical views of Willard Van Orman Quine.

In chapter 3, I move on to meatier topics. The empirical nature of Davidson's approach is placed in relief through an analysis of various theories of reference. I argue that from Davidson's perspective, causal and intensionalist theories of reference suffer from the same kind of defect. This defect is fatal; I conclude that no theory of reference can ever serve as the foundation of a theory of meaning.

The import of Davidson's holistic view of the source of the empirical content of a semantic theory is brought out in chapter 4, where the traditional notion of truth as correspondence is contrasted with Alfred Tarski's concept of *satisfaction*. Still, both concepts appear to involve some relationship between language and the world. Does this make Davidson's semantics an underpinning for realism? It does not, I argue, at least on any traditional understanding of realism.

The idea of satisfaction is essential to Davidson's theoretical machinery because it is the key to Tarski's definition of truth. And this definition provides, according to Davidson, the structure of a theory of interpretation. But Tarski's definition works only for formalized languages. How can Tarski's theory be applied to natural languages? This question is addressed in the first part of chapter 5. The remainder of the chapter is an attempt to justify the claim that a theory of truth for a natural language is an interpretation of that language. I discuss the relation between the truth conditions of sentences and the meanings of sentences, as well as the significance of the theoretical constraints imposed by Tarski's convention T, that is, his test of the adequacy of a theory of truth for a given language. The discussion is intended to challenge the commonly held view that constraints other than truth are needed to eliminate apparently absurd theories.

Chapters 6 and 7 are concerned with the nature of the empirical content of theories formulated in accordance with convention T: What are the assumptions we must make if observations are to provide an evidential base from which we can inductively axiomatize a theory and against which the theory can be tested? How constraining is the empirical evidence? Through the answers to these questions, the full significance of the concept of truth for Davidson's view of language will begin to emerge. Against current orthodoxy, I claim that in interpreting speakers we maximize the empirical content of our theories solely by construing speakers as speakers of truth. There is no need to bring in psychological or other principles as constraints on our theories of interpretation.

In chapter 8, I show how Davidson's articulation of his understanding of the explanatory function of the concept of truth finally leads him to reject the very idea of a language as a semantically uninformative concept. However, I argue, this move is precipitous. For while Davidson is right to conclude that linguistic understanding is not to be explicated in terms of knowing a language, the concept of a language can still be useful to our understanding of linguistic communication. But its usefulness depends on our assigning to the notion of a language a new function in our explanatory strategies.

The ambitious intent of these closely related discussions is to provide both an idea of what language is and an account of how we use it to communicate. Thus armed, I will, in chapter 9, be in a position to give an analysis of incommensurability in which this concept, like that of truth, will turn out to be an essential element in a dialectic of critical, reflexive interpretation.

NOTES

1 Most of these papers are collected in Davidson, D. (1984), *Inquiries into Truth and Interpretation*, Clarendon Press, hereafter cited as *Inquiries*.

2
What is a Theory of Truth?

At first careless glance, it might appear misleading to construe Davidson as attempting to provide a theory of meaning. His work in semantics is informed by Quine's scepticism towards 'meanings', and is directed towards the possibility of constructing a theory of truth for natural languages. Davidson finds the basic model for such theories in the work of Tarski, who showed us how to construct a theory of truth for formalized languages.[1] But unlike Tarski, who sought and found a way to define the concept of truth, Davidson's goal is not simply a characterization of this notion. He is not primarily interested in Tarski's semantic concern, which was to find a way of expressing what we mean by calling a sentence true. And he is certainly not attempting to construct an epistemological or metaphysical theory of truth in the sense of a theory about the *nature* of truth.[2] Davidson's question is, 'what is it for words to mean what they do?' (*Inquiries*, p. xiiv). The answer amounts to a 'theory of meaning', which for Davidson is 'not a technical term but a gesture in the direction of a family of problems (a problem family)' (*Inquiries*, p. 215).

If it is to avoid circularity, a theory of meaning must explain communication without relying on undefined semantic concepts.[3] To do that, it must fulfil two basic requirements: it must be powerful enough to provide an interpretation of any utterance a speaker of a natural language might make, and it must be testable against evidence available independently of any knowledge of the linguistic concepts of the language (see for instance *Inquiries*,

p. xiiv or p. 215). The thrust of Davidson's reflections on language is that these demands are satisfied by a Tarski-style theory of truth. Theories of truth are the focus of Davidson's investigations in so far as they give the structure of a theory of meaning.

Accordingly, there are two clusters of problems around which the bulk of his work in semantics is spun: the first centres around the question, how can a theory of truth provide us with a theory of meaning? The best-known and most accessible of Davidson's papers on language revolve around this problem. The first cluster has two main aspects, corresponding to the two demands he places on a philosophically interesting explanation of communication: one has to do with how a theory of truth yields interpretations of statements, and another with what is required of such a theory for it to be empirically testable.

The second cluster of problems surrounds the question, how can a theory of truth for a natural language be constructed? Here we are in the domain of the more technical questions, questions that concern, in effect, the actual subjugation of language to the technology of quantification. Davidson's contributions to this process are significant, but since I am concerned more with the philosophical underpinnings and consequences of his strategy than with the mechanics of the strategy itself, I shall pass by in relative silence those papers that deal with the specific logical structure of things like adverbial attribution, quotation and indirect speech.

How does the kind of theory that Tarski constructed tell us what we mean by calling a sentence true? Essentially by recursively characterizing a set of sentences that give the truth-conditions for all the indicative sentences of a language. We may, in other words, regard the structural model provided by Tarski for Davidson's theories of meaning as theories that give the extension of the truth-predicate for a given language. In putting it this way, two important points emerge: the first is simply that there is no *one* theory of truth. Not only is there no one theory of truth for all languages, but, it will turn out, in the case of natural languages there is no way even to uniquely determine the extension of the truth-predicate for any particular language. Or, more felicitously, we might say that we can never uniquely determine the language to which an utterance belongs, a predicament from which we should take conceptual warning. The difference between these formulations is significant, and bears directly on the nature of the indeterminacy of translation. It also contains the seeds of suspicion towards the concept of a language.

The second fundamental point is this: the task of constructing a theory which gives the extension of the truth-predicate of a language is the task of showing how, from a finite number of axioms and procedural rules, we can deduce the infinite number of theorems that give the truth-conditions for the sentences of the language. This is no mean feat; it presupposes, for instance, at least on Davidson's view, that we can extend first-order logic horizontally in such a way that we can capture the logical structure of any possible kind of assertion in a language in quantificational terms.[4] But it is a very different feat from the one of providing a theory of that elusive something by virtue of which true sentences are true. The distinction is essential, and should be obvious. The problem is that both kinds of theories might sloppily be glossed as theories about what makes sentences true (cf. *Inquiries*, p. 70). So, at the risk of belabouring the point, let me put it this way: Davidson's kind of theory is one which would enable us to specify the conditions under which a sentence in a language is true, without telling us anything about when those conditions prevail or how to determine whether they do prevail. It is a semantic theory, and as such is about how we use language. As a theory of truth, specifically, it gives a systematic account of the restrictions that must be brought to bear upon our use of any given sentence of a language if we are to call that sentence true. For Davidson, the only property true sentences have in common is the property of being used in accordance with these restrictions. Conversely, the attempt to construct an account of truth on the basis of a purported relation between sentences and something else is, in a sense that will become clearer in chapter four, like pressing the accelerator when the car is in neutral. As explanatory vehicles, such theories are not going anywhere.

This is not to say that we should not have theories about how we come to believe that the truth-conditions for a given sentence or set of sentences do in fact prevail, or about how we can justify such beliefs. These are theories of perception, observation, learning and communication; they treat of psychology, neurology and biology, of sociology and history. The one thing they are not about is *truth*. The elucidation of the concept of truth is a matter of semantics. Judging the truth-value of sentences is a matter of human inquiry running the gamut from idle speculation and loose observation to rigorous, explicitly systematic cognitive procedures. Epistemology, in so far as it is simply such inquiry directed towards itself, is just part of our normative theorizing about how to justify our beliefs; how to make our inquiries as efficient as possible in establishing the truth-value of sentences. Here is where, for instance, theories about the possibility of verification and falsification, about surface irritations and *qualia* find their place, but such theories are not the only, perhaps not even the primary, kind of theory that is epistemological in this broad and innocuous sense. Trouble arises only when epistemology conflates the question of what it is for a sentence to be true (which asks what we mean by calling a sentence true), with the question of how we know whether a sentence *is* true. This is where epistemology becomes the search for certainty, founded on the misconception that there is just one answer to the second question and that an answer to the first will provide it. This is the mistake of thinking that if we only stare at the concept of truth sufficiently hard for a sufficiently long time, we will crack its riddle and thus recognize its mark on all true sentences. Armed with this mark, with cartesian insight into the nature of truth itself independent of our investigations into particular matters of fact, we would be able to specify justificatory criteria for our beliefs about the world in terms that are primary with respect to our inquiry into how things are. But if we keep the two questions about truth properly distinct, we must abandon this idea of a riddle of truth. And with it, we must abandon the distinction between legitimizing accounts of knowledge and genealogical accounts of knowledge. What we are left with is, on the one hand, epistemology naturalized, and on the other, semantics.

Avoiding the confusion implicit in the notion of something *making* sentences true, something in virtue of the possession of which sentences fall into natural classes like 'true' and 'false', hinges on our keeping semantics distinct from epistemology. Only then will we be able to appreciate the nature of the key issue of verifiability. A semantic theory of truth is verifiable, it will turn out, precisely because it allows us to 'characterize the property of truth without having to find entities to which sentences that have the property differentially correspond' (*Inquiries*, p. 70). Only then will we appreciate in what sense and to what extent Davidson relies on a pre-theoretical grasp of truth in order to forge a theory of meaning out of a semantic theory of truth.

In formulating a theory of meaning on the basis of Tarski's answer to the question of what it is for a sentence to be true, Davidson assumes that we have some answers to the second question of how to determine the truth-value of sentences. In a peculiar way, he might also be said to contribute to our faith in those answers. But he is no epistemologist; he does not deal in that currency, though many cheques have been written in his name.

The search for the mark of truth in the form of entities to which sentences can correspond is a venerable tradition, the continuation of which is possible only for someone unimpressed by Quine's efforts to undermine the distinction between questions of meaning and questions of the way of the world. Ever since the early 1950s and the publication of 'Two Dogmas of Empiricism' (Quine, 1961), Quine has been making the point that when we pursue our conceptual truths genealogically, following their roots towards the source of their presumed special status, we do not make the expected discovery of empirically uncontaminated meaning. Instead we find only unquestioned agreement, of just the kind that prevails about the more obvious features of the world. The difference between questions of meaning and questions of fact amounts to a difference in degree of consensus, or, in those cases where consensus is strong, to the sorts of conclusions we tend to draw about anyone who refuses to conform. We might defend our consensus against the non-conformist by recommending a sensory-apparatus examination, or by suggesting a remedial course in English. Quine argues that this difference in our response towards a deviant is not in the end supported by an underlying difference in the kinds of question at issue.

Quine's point is best appreciated in the context of his holistic critique of verificationism. He agrees that meaning does lie in the difference made by something's being the case: As the verificationists maintained, the meaning of some bit of language is to be explicated in terms of the sensory givens that would lead us to assent to that bit of language. The problem is that the sort of thing we assent to, that is, sentences, cannot individually be brought into determinate relations with packets of sense data or patterns of stimulation or any other such attempted explication of the given. This is one of the key points in 'Epistemology Naturalized' (Quine, 1969b). Quine argues in this essay that 'the typical statement about bodies has no fund of experiential implications it can call its own ... [only a] substantial mass of theory, taken together, will commonly have experiential implications; this is how we make verifiable predictions' (Quine, 1969b, p. 79). This holistic approach to the confrontation of language with experience eliminates the possibility of distinguishing between a contribution of meaning and a contribution of the world towards making our sentences true or false. The reason is that it leaves us no isolable thing that corresponds to the idea of 'the meaning of a sentence' in the sense required. If we equate meaning with empirical content, as Quine does, and insist that only theories as wholes have empirical content, then sentences have meaning only as parts of a body of theory. In such a body it is possible to systematically tamper with the roles assigned to its parts, words and sentences, in ways that leave the empirical content of the theory as a whole unaltered. This is Quine's doctrine of the indeterminacy of translation. As Davidson stresses, 'it should be viewed as neither mysterious nor threatening. It is no more mysterious than the fact that temperature can be measured in Centigrade or Fahrenheit' (Davidson, 1986b, p. 313). Different ways of translating a speaker into some other language can be equally satisfactory because of the asymmetrical relation between truth and empirical content entailed by Quine's holistic view of meaning: While we ascribe truth-values to individual sentences, we ascribe definite empirical content only to bodies of sentences. Indeterminacy of translation is the free play resulting from the fact that it is always possible to neutralize the effects of alterations in the truth-value of one sentence on the body as a whole by making adjustments elsewhere. This asymmetry in the ascription of meaning and truth is also what deprives the analytic − synthetic distinction of any grip. In criticizing the distinction, Quine is arguing not that we cannot make sense of the concepts of analytic and synthetic sentences, he is suggesting that these classes of sentences are empty. As Dummett points out in 'The Significance of Quine's Indeterminacy Thesis' (Dummett, 1978):

> [Quine's position is that] an analytic sentence is one such that no recalcitrant experience would lead us to withdraw our assignment to it of the value true, while a synthetic one is such that any adequate revision prompted by certain recalcitrant experiences would involve our withdrawing our assignment to it of the value true ... as thus defined, there are no analytic sentences, and there are no synthetic ones. (Dummett, 1978, pp. 375).

The reason is the implication that even while we ascribe definite empirical content to a body of sentences, we are unable to secure any individual sentence in that body against possible revision. In short, Quine argues that it is impossible to fix the meaning of any individual sentence by reference to experience.

Quine's holism undermines any attempt to give privileged status to certain kinds of truth. Giving up the two dogmas of empiricism, the dogmas of analyticity and reductionism, means, first, that we can no longer retreat to a special class of sentences the truth of which are guaranteed by virtue of their meaning. And giving up foundational epistemology in the face of 'the impossibility of strictly deriving the science of the external world from sensory evidence' (Quine, 1969b, p. 75), and even of translating all of science into sentences about sensory evidence, means that there is no hope of isolating a special class of sentences the truth of which is guaranteed by virtue of the way the world is. Meaning is no more nor less definite than empirical content, and neither can be ascribed to sentences regarded in isolation. Truth, on the other hand, as a property of individual sentences, is never fully constrained by the empirical content or meaning that we ascribe to bodies of sentences. Once the point is made that the domains of the concepts of truth and meaning are not defined at the same level of linguistic structure, it becomes clear that neither semantics nor epistemology can provide us with a firm foundationalist footing. Truths about language are no more immutable than truths about empirical inquiry, and truths about empirical inquiry are no less subject to revision than truths of such inquiry.

On Davidson's account it is impossible to overestimate the significance of Quine's prying loose the concept of meaning from individual sentences, that is, from the vehicles of truth. Davidson writes: 'In my view, erasing the line between the analytic and synthetic saved philosophy of language as a serious subject by showing how it could be pursued without what there cannot be: determinate meanings' (Davidson, 1986b, p. 313). But he adds: 'I now suggest also giving up the distinction between observation sentences and the rest' (Davidson, 1986b, p. 313). Observation sentences or occasion sentences are Quine's version of the sensory given. Quine, true to his naturalism, regards occasion sentences as defined with relation to a given speaker or group of speakers. The trained scientist's occasion sentence will be the young student's inference. But no matter how fluidly construed, they are meant to serve as the link to experience that ultimately grounds our knowledge claims. For Quine, observation sentences are thus endowed with a special – and central – epistemological status. This is what makes Quine an empiricist, and it is precisely what Davidson means to challenge, for example, in 'A Coherence Theory of Truth and Knowledge' (Davidson, 1986b), and most recently in 'Meaning, Truth and Evidence' (Davidson, 1988).[5]

Quine refuses to regard sentences, taken individually, and the world as the *relata* of a relation either in need of or susceptible to philosophical grounding over and above the various forms of our inquiry into the nature of things. But he stops short of rejecting the whole idea of an epistemologically significant relation between language and experience. The myth of the given survives in Quine's writings in the form of the idea that sensations not only cause beliefs, but can somehow justify them. The concept of occasion sentences is an attempt to harness sensations for justificatory purposes.[6] For Davidson, this is an impossible task. Only beliefs can justify beliefs; the only *evidence* there can be for the truth of a sentence are other true sentences.

Quine never draws this conclusion, and his failing to do so is the source of most of his disagreements with Davidson. Quine himself criticized the epistemological attempt to wash the dye out of the grey texture of language in order to separate it into the white of meaning and the black of fact. And at the heart of Davidson's semantic strategy is the Quinian insight that we can never get truth by squeezing the concept of meaning; truth and falsehood are properties of sentences, and as such uniquely compound. For the purpose of testing not just our theories about the way the world is, but our theories about words and how they come to mean, we must treat grey as a primary colour. But Davidson presses Quine's critique of empiricism to its conclusion by exposing Quine's notion of occasion sentences as a vestige of the attempt to isolate some ultimate source of evidence for our beliefs, some special class of sentences that are not grey, but white or black. We do not need an epistemological bridge between language and the world, Davidson insists, because 'language is not a filter or a screen through which knowledge of the world must pass' (*Inquiries*, p. xvii). We transcend verificationism only when we abandon the metaphor of epistemological confrontation between language and the world altogether. This we do when we realize that while experience causes us to hold sentences true, it does not *make* sentences true, neither individually nor as corporate bodies.

> Nothing ... no *thing*, makes sentences and theories true: not experience, not surface irritations, not the world, can make a sentence true. *That* experience takes a certain course ... make[s] sentences and theories true. (*Inquiries*, p. 194)

NOTES

1 By a formalized language, Tarski means one for which a list is given in what he calls 'structural-descriptive terms' of 'all the signs with which the expressions of the language are formed ... [and in which] ... among all possible expressions which can be formed with these signs those called sentences are distinguished by means of purely structural properties' (Tarski, 1956, p. 166).
2 In 'The Method of Truth in Metaphysics', in *Inquiries*, (pp. 199–214), Davidson proposes not a metaphysical theory of truth but suggests, on the contrary, that an empirical theory of truth will serve as a basis for metaphysical investigations.
3 Which is not to make the impossible demand that a theory of meaning does not employ semantic concepts. The point is simply the obvious one that the theory cannot assume an understanding of concepts like 'meaning', 'translation', and so on.
4 Though Davidson does believe that a theory of truth would accommodate other logics, he has argued that the fact that first-order quantification theory is complete constitutes a strong argument for relying on it as far as possible.

5 In 'Meaning, Truth and Evidence' (delivered at the Quine Conference, St Louis, April 1988), Davidson clarifies the relation between Quine's notion of observation sentences and his empiricist commitments. Davidson argues that Quine should give up his official theory of meaning — a 'proximal' one, in Davidson's terminology, which defines sameness of meaning for observation sentences in terms of sameness of patterns of stimuli, and so in terms of something private — in favour of a 'distal' theory which defines sameness of meaning in terms of public objects and events. This would, according to Davidson, save Quine from the relativism of truth and the scepticism of the senses that seem inescapably to flow from empiricism in its various guises, without jeopardizing his naturalism.

6 For the suggestion that Quine remains attached to the myth of the given, see Rorty (1979, p. 171). See also Davidson (1986b, particularly pp. 311–13).

3
Reference

On Quine's holistic view of meaning — or, as Quine would have it, on his holistic elimination of meaning — the constraints imposed by the empirical content of a body of sentences are in principle insufficient to uniquely determine the semantic roles of the sentential or word-constituents of that body. If this is true, no analysis of 'meaning' will ever determine reference. Conversely, nor could an account of how the sentences or words of language hook up with the world ever provide us with a theory of meaning.

The assumption of a strong connection between meaning and reference, however, is fundamental to classical theories of meaning: To know the meaning or sense of a word is to know how to pick out its referent. And once reference is secure, we are on the road to truth, that is, in a position to spell out the truth-conditions of sentences. Or so the theories go. To this picture, on which reference is central to an account of both truth and meaning, Davidson opposes his holistic conception of language. As he shifts the focus from epistemology to semantics, Davidson drops Quine's vestigial empiricism. As a result, the concept of reference passes from inscrutability to obscurity. Davidson turns upside down the traditional approach to truth and meaning, and in the process deprives the idea of reference of any useful semantic purpose.

It is not just classical theories that are cut off from their foundations as a result of Davidson's inversion. In the present chapter, I shall argue that the two fundamentally different theories of meaning and reference (and the endless proliferation of variations on the two themes) which have emerged over the last 20 or so years – partly causing and partly resulting from the demise of the classical theories – are subject to the same sorts of consideration that render the classical approach circular from Davidson's point of view. What Davidson shows is that reference, whether intensionally or causally construed, can never be made to support the conceptual weight of a theory of interpretation.

A prominent theorist of language, J. J. Katz, attributes to the classical theories of meaning the thesis that 'knowledge of the meaning of a word is the basis on which speakers use it to refer' (Katz, 1979, p. 103). The modern version of the classical conception was launched by Gottlob Frege's 'On Sense and Reference' (1962) and 'it has been developed and defended by [in addition to Frege] . . . Church, C.I. Lewis, Carnap, and Searle' (Katz, 1979, p. 103). (Katz does not mention Bertrand Russell, though he probably should have.) What is shared by these theorists is, in the words of Howard Wettstein, 'the idea that singular terms express descriptive concepts and refer to those items that satisfy the concepts' (Wettstein, 1984, p. 63).

The formulations of Katz and Wettstein articulate the same fundamental point, which is at the heart of the Fregean tradition and the root of its trouble: on Frege's theory, fixing the reference of a given expression presupposes an account of its sense or meaning that is prior to the way in which the expression is actually used. Without an account specifying the sense of an expression in advance, there is no way to tell, in any particular instance of its use, whether it successfully refers. The notion of analyticity is only of apparent help here. In the end, Frege and his philosophical successors are unable to escape a rather small circle of 'logical truths' defined as truths by virtue of sense alone and 'sense' as whatever it is that makes analytic truths true. The point is highlighted in the case of proper names: How do names refer? By expressing something true of their objects, the classic answer goes. But what truth or set of truths? How do we decide whether we are misinformed about one person or object or actually talking about another? Which truths about Jones are accidental and which are essential to Jones being Jones? In a short discussion of Moses and an even shorter one of chairs, Ludwig Wittgenstein popularized the sport of ridiculing the idea that any such set could ever be specified (cf. Wittgenstein, 1958, pp. 36e–38e). This line of attack has since been pursued with particular success by Hilary Putnam and Saul Kripke.[1] The basic strategy is to take any proposed list and dream up examples where either the list is satisfied even though we would want to say the noun (proper or common) fails to refer, or the list is not satisfied even though we would want to insist that reference succeeds. One might feel that no general conclusion follows from such intuitive counter-examples, but then they are merely meant to illustrate the crucial point that any a priori legislation on meaning of the kind required by a description theory of reference would be just that, legislation. Being stipulative in nature, such legislation could not explain how words come to refer in the ways they actually do refer, or how they come to have the meanings they do have.

The *locus classicus* of the death certificate of the attempt to derive reference from description is Keith Donnellan's 'Proper Names and Identifying Descriptions' (Donnellan, 1972), published along with Kripke's 'Naming and Necessity' (Kripke, 1972). The reason for this is not the originality of his arguments against the classical theory, which effectively show that the classical theory does not command the conceptual resources to hold sense and reference sufficiently far apart to examine any relationship between them. The arguments are not essentially different from those presented (or hinted at) by Wittgenstein, Kripke or Putnam, or by Donnellan himself in earlier papers (see for instance Donnellan, 1962; or Donnellan, 1966). The reason is that Donnellan not only drew the fatal circle, he greatly facilitated the acceptance of the passing of the classical account by providing an alternative strategy:

> On the positive side my view is that what we should substitute for the question, 'What is the referent?' is 'What would the speaker be attributing that predicate to on this occasion?' ... *How* we answer such questions I do not have a general theory about. It seems clear to me that in some way the referent must be historically, or, we might say, causally connected to the speech act. But I do not see my way clear to saying exactly how in general the connection goes. Perhaps there is no exact theory. (Donnellan, 1972, p. 377)

Thus, timidly, was born the causal theory of reference. The causal theory attempts to explain the power of words (or other semantic tokens) to refer to objects in terms of causal chains involving the objects and our linguistic representations of them. Whether, say, a singular term designates a particular object then becomes a question of whether the appropriate causal links hold between the object and our use of the term. The attractions of such a theory are obvious. It can be embedded in a more general theory of representation, a project D. W. Stampe sketches in 'Toward a Causal Theory of Linguistic Representation' (Stampe, 1979). Such a theory, he writes, 'seems to promise not only a unified treatment of the various object-involving phenomena [knowledge, memory, belief, evidence, etc.], but a naturalistic and possibly even physicalistic one as well' (Stampe, 1979, p. 87).

It is also possible, of course, to embrace a causal account of reference while resisting the idea that reference can thus be naturalistically or physicalistically construed. Kripke, for instance, has taken this position right from the start. It seems, though, that much of the recent support for a causal account of reference – such as that offered by Jerry Fodor, Michael Devitt and Hartry Field, among others (see Fodor, 1987; Devitt, 1981, 1985; Field, 1972, 1975, 1978) – has been motivated precisely by what is perceived as a promise of a semantics compatible with physicalism.

What a causal theory of reference requires is nothing less than a schema for a description of causal relations such that, in Fodor's words, 'it provides a sufficient condition for one part of the world to be semantically related to another part' (Fodor, 1987, p. 126).

Since any representation is involved in many ways in as many kinds of causal relations to the world, this is no small task. It will not, of course, do simply to provide a list of causal chains that actually happen to run between referent and that which refers, no matter how many cases of successful reference is incorporated in the generalization. What is needed to *account for* this success is a counterfactual-supporting theory; a causal theory of reference must tell us what the reference of a term *would* be, *were* certain causal relations to hold (see Fodor, 1987, p. 99). It must, in other words, represent the causal relations between representation and referent nomologically. For a semantic theory in which the generalizations are not lawlike, has no predictive power, and without predictive power, we have no explanation of anything. So, then, as Stampe writes, the causal theorist 'must find a way to associate the concepts of accuracy and expression with natural processes or properties — that is, probably, with the natural processes that underlie *the lawful relationships that hold between features of representations and features of things represented*' (Stampe, 1979, pp. 87–8) [my italic]. This task is complicated, to say the least, by the fact that 'whether an English word gets tokened ... depends not just on what it means but also upon the motivations, linguistic competences, and communicative intentions of English speakers. Giving voice to an utterance, unlike entertaining a thought, is typically a voluntary act.' (Fodor, 1987, p. 100) A route that looks like it might circumvent this problem — one recommended by Devitt, Field and Fodor among many others — goes by way of a particular position in the philosophy of mind. What needs to be explained, on this view, is the intentionality of mental representations; the locus of semantic power is not the language we speak, it is the *language of thought* (see Devitt, 1981, pp. 75–80; Fodor, 1975, 1987, particularly pp. 135–54; Field, 1978). Our ability to use natural language to represent or refer to features of the world is construed as derivative, the *explanandum* of the theory is thus shifted out of the nomologically troublesome realm of voluntary speech acts.

The idea of a language of thought is hotly debated within the philosophy of mind, and within cognitive science in general. In the present context, I am concerned only with what purchasing power the idea has for an empirical semantics; I discuss it simply because it seems to me that the strongest recent cases for causal theories of reference make use of the notion. The distinguishing feature of LOT, as Fodor has dubbed it, 'is the idea that ... mental states that have content also have syntactic structure — constituent structure in particular — that's appropriate to the content they have' (Fodor, 1987, p. 137). In so far as they are intentional realists, LOT advocates hold that our hopes, beliefs, fears and wants are bona fide elements of an account of what there is in the world. They are not first-order physical properties, but functional states, purportedly characterizable as relations to physical tokens of symbols with intentional content. That such symbols with intentional content — roughly, *what* we believe, fear, hope, or desire — are complex, is taken for granted. But

LOT implies not only that the objects of intentional states are complex; LOT entails that our mental states themselves have syntactic structure.

LOT happens to combine two features which are both essential to the causal theorist: Firstly, LOT appears to make possible the specification of causal chains and webs which tie together the semantic constituents of a language and features of the world in the law-like connections that a causal theory of reference requires, but that the voluntary nature of our speech acts seems to block. While we as speakers of English can choose, say, to refrain from remarking upon the egg on the speaker's chin, we cannot, once we spot it, simply *choose* not to *think* that there is egg on the speaker's chin. In *mentalese* we are helplessly indiscrete. And it is precisely because we cannot help ourselves — that is, because thought is not, as Fodor says, voluntary — that there might appear to be some hope of characterizing a predicate true of all and only those occasions when we cannot but token a particular *mentalese* expression.

However, if thoughts did not have constituent structure, this possibility would be of no use to the semanticist; we can presumably think any number of thoughts, and a theory which would require an axiom for each of them would be no theory at all. So the second feature of LOT is essential: like natural-language expressions, *mentalese* expressions can *ex hypothesis* be generated from a finite stock of primitive expressions and combinatorial rules, so that the meaning of a complex expression can be construed as a function of the meaning of its semantic constituents. And this means that the content of an infinite variety of thoughts can be captured by a finite set of axioms, which give semantic content to the finite basic vocabulary in terms of causal relations, and to any complex expression in terms of combinatorial rules.

Introducing LOT, then, is a way of breaking down the problem faced by the proponents of the causal theory into something more manageable. What is needed, firstly, is a schema giving the form of laws that causally relate some property of the world to the tokening of some semantic type. Here is where the LOT hypothesis does its work; since *mentalese* tokenings — thoughts — are beyond our control in a way our speech acts are not, their etiology is presumably susceptible to law-like generalizations of a kind that the etiology of speech acts escape. Secondly, we need an account of the relation between natural language and the language of thought; of how it is that the representational power of expressions of *mentalese* enables us to refer to features of the world by using, for example, English. To give such an account would *ipso facto* be to suggest how our use of natural language might lend evidential support to a particular semantic interpretation of the language of thought, that is, to a particular assignment of referents to *mentalese* expressions.

The first part of the problem has attracted most of the creative labour of the causal theorists. No wonder; without a plausible way of framing a description of the kinds of causal connection between representations and things that determine the semantic value of our referring expressions, there would be no causal conception of reference to argue about. What is required here, as Fodor stresses, is not a description of this or that particular causal route, but a description which *quantifies over* the various causal connections between the tokenings of an expression and its referent, preserving their *covariance*. The catalogue of difficulties is familiar; how to accommodate opaque contexts, where the substitution of coreferential terms changes the truth-value of a sentence; how to cope with ambiguities, empty terms, fictitious names, and so on; how to explain the fact that symbols cannot always be taken to express what appears to cause their tokenings (that is, how to account for mistakes in our descriptions and designations). These problems have at various times given rise to purported counter-examples to suggested causal characterizations of reference, examples of causal connections which fit some particular characterization of reference but which appear to tie together semantic types and parts of the world in intuitively implausible ways. But there is no reason to suppose that the explication of the predicate 'refers to' − or rather, of the various predicates ('designates', 'denotes', 'applies to', and the like) that describe the different kinds of reference − cannot be modified to absorb such counter-examples. As long as there is no constraint on the explication of the predicates other than our intuitions about reference, such counter-examples will never defeat the program, they will only contribute to the refinement of the theory.

However, in this, I think, lies a hint of the sorts of considerations that might contribute to the defeat of the general approach, not just of particular versions of it. For it suggests that there is a problem in the relation between theories of reference and the kind of evidence we can have for semantic theories.

The natural way to go about testing a theory of reference for our mental representations would be to presume that our language of thought is pretty much like the language we speak (or write or sign or whatever), and then find a way of testing a semantic interpretation of this language. This is Devitt's approach (see Devitt, 1981, pp. 75–6), which looks like it might side-step the problem of explicating the relation between the language of thought and the language we speak. Identifying a person's 'public language' (as Devitt calls it) with their language of thought preserves the advantage essential to the causal theorist which stems from the fact that as thinkers we are more regular and predictable than we are as speakers. At the same time, it appears to do away with the obligation to provide a story about the relation between the language of thought and the thinker's public language. What happens, in effect, is this: to explain the meaning of natural language expressions, we postulate a language of thought. We do this, because there seems to be a better chance of informative causal generalizations applying to the tokenings of a language of thought than to our public utterances. Then, for the purposes of *testing* these generalizations, we shift *back* to the domain of natural languages, thus, presumably, preserving the connection between the postulated language of thought and whatever empirical evidence can be had for a particular semantic interpretation of the language. This is clever, but I don't see how it can work. Here is why.

In testing an actual theory of meaning for a language, rather than a description of a theory of meaning, we want to know if a specific set of causal generalizations are true. So the question is, how would we go about testing a particular causal theory?

Let us imagine that we have come up with a candidate for a schema giving the form of the sorts of nomological generalizations we think we want. Let us imagine, too, that we have produced a theory in which the axioms are generalizations that accord with this schema, a theory which produces theorems that assign referents to terms. The question is: Against what do we test these theorems of a causal theory? How do we distinguish implausible from plausible generalizations of the causal determinations of the reference of a term? It might appear that the empirical content of a causal theory is provided by the causal chains it picks out between an expression and an object. For surely whether or not a given kind of chain obtains is an empirical matter of fact; we could, so to speak, look and see. But the particular causal links between the referring expression and its referent can only be taken to specify the reference of the expression if the causal law of which it is an instantiation is known to be true. And this is just the question we are asking: how do we know that *this* causal chain or *that* causal web are the ones that we shold quantify over in determining the semantic value of an expression? How do we know, that is to say, that our theory is a good one?

It is no answer to point out that we have got the form of the nomological generalizations right. For the formulation of the schema, which supposedly applies to the language of thought and which provides this form, takes for granted our semantic intuitions; it is based on generalizations of our semantic intuitions in cases where we are confident, on grounds independent of the theory, that we know how the relation of reference goes. But now we stand, *ex hypothesis*, without such semantic intuitions; what we are after is an interpretation of a particular language, or, if we like, a particular speaker's thoughts. How do we know that we are looking for the right kinds of causal connections in this particular case? Well, in general we know that causal generalizations apply because there are ways of telling whether their predictions are true, ways that are available to us whether we know the law or not. So to test a theory about reference-determining causal chains, we need to determine the referents of expressions in a way that does not presuppose semantic intuitions about the language for which we are trying to formulate a theory. We need a way of verifying whether the speaker (or thinker) of that language actually has the thoughts that our causal hypotheses would attribute to her.

A causal *theory* of reference, a set of hypotheses concerning the causal chains that define the semantic values of the expressions of a given language, must be tested against the *actual* reference of the expressions in its domain. But how does a causal theorist unpack the relevant evidential base? Only, it would seem to any post-Fregean theorist, in terms of sentences held true or false. A plausible causal theory of reference would be one that postulated causal relations between objects and representations that mapped words to objects in a way that left the truth-values of our sentences pretty well as they are. Indeed, Devitt himself makes this clear when he justifies a particular feature of his theory of designation by saying that his 'motive in ruling out transmission of benefits in these cases is simply to get the intuitively right answer at the level of truth values' (Devitt, 1981, p. 149).

In this case, it looks as though a theory of reference has empirical content in the sense that it *explains* how words refer the way they do only if we have available a notion of truth which is independent of that theory. A theory of reference, tested against an unanalysed concept of truth, might serve as an explication of (at least a subset of) the intuitions that constitute our knowing a language. But what we want is a theory that interprets a language we do not already understand. Now we might think that the causal theory would allow us, at least in principle, to do this; feeding particular expressions into it, we get referents falling out as products of the nomological causal generalizations that constitute the theory. But the problem is that unless we understand the language, we have no criteria for identifying those causal relations that are relevant to semantic content. Out of the indeterminate number of possible causal links between words and objects we could simply pick certain instances as the bases for generalization, but our selections would be arbitrary. We can certainly come up with a causal theory of reference for a language we know, but in applying the form of these generalizations to cases where we have no intuitions to bear them out, the body of our theory would be mere legislation, without empirical content.

The essential point is that when we confront a language we do not understand, we cannot know if our theory isolates the *appropriate* set of causal laws. The evidence against which a set can be tested is only available to someone who understands the language.

It would be a mistake to grant this point while thinking of causal theories as having semantically relevant empirical content in those cases where the language is understood. The empirical hypotheses such theories would allow us to frame are etymological hypotheses about how the words we use might have come to mean what they do. This is no doubt an interesting topic in its own right, but to cast light on it is not to illuminate any semantic terrain.

A reference theorist would no doubt protest. After all, in *Psychosemantics* (1987) Fodor provides a sustained and detailed argument for the view that we can describe in non-semantic terms the causal connections that are purported to determine reference (see Fodor, 1987, p. 126). But the point I want to make is not that this is impossible, but that for the purposes of a theory of the interpretation of a language, this is not enough. For the issue that must be empirical on such a theory is precisely whether these descriptions actually do capture reference. And to settle this question, we would need to be able to describe in non-semantic terms independently testable consequences of the causal generalizations that make up the theory. This is what cannot be done. Without begging the question at issue − without, that is, assuming that our reference-assigning causal theory is true − the only way to find out whether a particular expression refers to a particular object is to see how that term affects the truth-value of the sentences in which it occurs.

Devitt, for one, resists the semantic dependence of reference on a concept of truth:

> The Davidsonians are of course right to emphasize that the evidence for a semantic explanation is at the level of sentences. But it remains as mysterious to me now as it did before ... how this supports the view that truth, but not reference, is a place of 'direct contact between linguistic theory and events, actions or objects described in nonlinguistic terms' (Devitt, 1985, p. 170; the Davidson quote is from *Inquiries*, p. 219)

I think that this is mysterious to Devitt because, firstly, he appears to attribute a rather crude instrumentalism to Davidson, and, secondly, then goes on to argue that this instrumentalism does not 'justify discrimination against reference in favour of truth' (Devitt, 1985, p. 170). That the distinction 'between the "observational" sentences which are factual and the "theoretical" ones which are mere instruments' (Devitt, 1985, p. 169) does not support Davidson's position is not surprising. Fortunately, Davidson does not base his position on it. It would be odd if he did, since Davidson has done as much as anyone to advance the idea that a general distinction of this sort will support nothing at all.

The priority of truth over reference in semantics does not depend on a general instrumentalist distinction between observation statements and theoretical statements. What is required to support this priority is a distinction between the role of statements within a particular theory. And *with respect to a particular theory*, we can certainly distinguish between the kinds of statement that we rely on in testing the theory as a whole, and the kinds of statement that make up the structure of the theory. The former relates the concepts of a particular theory to concepts of other kinds, the latter defines the relationships between the concepts that the theory employs. It does not follow that we are committed to any notion of presuppositionless observation. The distinction Davidson relies on suggests that we test a theory in part by relating it to other (usually more general) sorts of theories. It definitely does not imply that the empirical consequences of a theory can somehow be tested directly against immediate experience, the given, or any such phantom. Certainly, as will become abundantly clear in the chapters on Radical Interpretation (chapters 6 and 7), in cashing the truth-value of sentences in non-semantic currency we rely, as Devitt claims, on 'a vast amount of theory' (Devitt, 1985, p. 169). But this vast amount of theory is not *semantic* theory. And that is what counts.

We cannot effect this exchange through a causal account of reference. While we might be able to *formulate* a causal theory of reference without using the concept of truth (or some similar predicate) *testing* such a theory presupposes knowledge of the truth-value of sentences, knowledge which we have come by independently of the theory to be tested. And our intuitions about the truth-values of sentences are certainly semantic, if anything is. If this is true, a causal theory of reference cannot give rise to the sorts of empirical predictions that we want a semantic theory to generate; they are always *ad hoc* explanations of meanings already known. The point can be put this way: if we know the extension of the truth-predicate of a language independently of our theory of reference, we at least have something against which to test our hypotheses about the causal relations between words, on the one hand, and objects and events on the other. But then, we do not need an independent theory of reference to understand the language, since, *ex hypothesi*, we already do. If, on the other hand, the causal theory is construed as a *foundation* for an account of truth, an account which describes an empirical causal relation between sentences and their extensions, the theory, *qua semantic* theory, gives up the only source of empirical content available to it by making this source a part of the theory itself.

The problem with the classical theory manifests itself in the fact that it must ascribe descriptive content to names in order to explain how they refer. The problem with the causal theory, Katz argues in defence of a very different conception of reference, is that:

> It adopts the use of proper nouns as the model of reference generally and accounts of the referential use of common nouns in accord with this model. Both theories assume that the reference of common nouns and the reference of proper nouns have a homogenous grammatical basis: meaning in the case of the classical theory, beliefs about the world in the case of the causal theory. (Katz, 1979, pp. 113–14)

While Katz agrees that names have no descriptive content, he insists that a theory of reference of common nouns must be given in intensional terms (see, for example, Katz, 1979 and 1986). The downfall of the classical theory was due to the 'inherent contradiction ... [between its] ... rationalist approach to meaning and its empiricist approach to language' (Katz, 1979, p. 105). Katz plausibly portrays the causal theory as the empiricist resolution of the contradiction. But the cost, he insists, perhaps less plausibly, is the counter-intuitive reduction of all sense to reference. So Katz purports to resolve the contradiction with a full-fledged rationalism, 'by adopting Chomsky's rationalist theory of grammatical structure' (Katz, 1979, p. 106). The neo-Kantian framework of a universal structure of language purportedly 'supplies the principles, missing in the classical theory, for distinguishing sense and reference, semantic structure and extralinguistic belief, meaning and use' (Katz, 1979, p. 106). The resulting theory is ingenious, and an internal critique of the fundamental project is impossible without taking on the Chomskyan enterprise. This I shall not attempt. The main point is that Katz's self-proclaimed neoclassical theory resolves the problems of its ancestor by not making any bones about relying on an a priori semantics. As a result, the theory purports to resurrect the analytic – synthetic distinction, concomitantly drawing a sharp line between semantic information (dictionary entries) and information about matters of fact (encyclopaedia entries), and to rehabilitate the claim that descriptive content is the source of reference for common nouns. The theory deflects counter-examples such as Wittgenstein's and Putnam's by relying on the distinction between 'type-reference' and 'token-reference', defining the former in terms of the meaning of a given expression, the latter in terms of the use of the expression in context (see Katz, 1979, p. 110; 1986, p. 64). So if, as Putnam imagines, cats turned out to be robotic spy-devices planted by Martians, 'cat' would fail to refer typally, and would always have failed to refer typally, but would successfully refer as token.[2] Once we see that sense determines type-reference but not token-reference, it is no longer possible 'to criticize necessity in language on the basis of contingency in the speech context' (Katz, 1986, p. 64).

Is this neoclassical theory a happy compromise? If we accept the Kantian – Chomskyan thesis to the effect that the structure of language is determined a priori by something like a linguistic central processing unit embedded in all speakers, that there is, so to speak, a *form* of linguistic rationality, then we can ground an account of purely semantic relations on the structural relations comprising that form. Neither analyticity nor type-reference would present us with definitional problems: Analytic truths reflect only the purely semantic structure of language; they contain only dictionary information. Since the dictionary is written independently of the encyclopaedia, sense is determined independently of the empirical history of the referring use of a given term. Hence, whether an expression type-refers to a given object is just a question of what properties the object manifests, as on the classical theory, but the classical circle is avoided. As for reference not determined by meaning, such as with names (or proper nouns), neoclassicists toss this bone to the causal theorists.[3] On Katz's account, the semantic circle is broken by tying intensionality to the common structure of all linguistic utterances, the Chomskyan a priori.

It is not just the fear of circularity, however, that has kept theorists of language from embracing intensionalist semantics. Davidson, speaking of belief sentences, remarks that 'we cannot account for even as much as the truth-conditions of such sentences on the basis of what we know of the meanings of the words in them' (*Inquiries*, p. 21). Katz, however, appears to have an answer. In 'Why Intensionalists Ought Not Be Fregeans', he aims to show that Benson Mates's famous criticism of 'Fregean criteria for inference by substitution into opaque contexts' (Katz, 1986, p. 60), such as belief sentences, is not damning to a more sophisticated intensionalist semantics.[4] This becomes apparent, Katz argues, once senses receive due attention and are not treated 'like humble servants who announce important personages under one or another of their titles' (Katz, 1986, p. 62). Mates's problem arises in contexts where truth is not preserved by the substitution of synonymous expressions. Frege suggested that in opaque contexts we consider the sense of an expression to be its referent, but this move, Mates points out, leaves Frege no way of blocking certain invalid inferences. What Katz shows is that this problem arises for Frege only because he pays insufficient attention to the workings of sense-compositionality, that is, the way in which 'the senses of sentences . . . [arise as] . . . a function of the senses of their syntactic constituents and the syntactic relations between these constituents' (Katz, 1986, p. 62). Abandoning what he calls a masonary conception of compositional structure, Katz suggests that the sense of the complement clause of, for instance, a propositional attitude verb can be altered by the verb operating on it. He labels verbs with this particular effect 'hyperopaque' (see Katz, 1986, p. 69). So for example, it is the hyperopacity of the verb 'believe' that explains why we cannot infer 'x believes that p' from 'x believes that p'' (where p and p' are synonymous): Because the senses of the complement clauses p and p' are altered by the verb, the two sentences need not have the same intentional object.

Katz contends that the relationship between the sense of a sentence and the senses of its parts is different in kind from that between a wall and the bricks in it. This is not implausible. And once we acknowledge that the senses of the constituents can be systematically transformed in the process of forming the sense of the sentence in which they occur, Katz's intensionalist solution to Mates's problem seems persuasive. Relying on the notion of hyperopacity, Katz can explain why 'x believes that p' and 'x believes that p''' have different truth-conditions. And then, as he says, 'both sides in this controversy are mistaken in supposing that Mates's problem has any relevance to the choice between intensionalism and extensionalism' (Katz, 1986, p. 61). But is intensionalism thus rehabilitated?

Perhaps, but only if we view the controversy as one between extensional and intensional theories of *reference*. But this is not the issue that divides Katz and Davidson. Katz writes as if Davidson's case against intensionalism rests solely on Mates's problem (see Katz, 1986, p. 60). I think this is false. From Davidson's point of view, Katz's intensionalism and what Katz takes to be the opposition, that is, extensional accounts of reference, share the same fundamental problem.

To stress the point yet again: a semantic theory has empirical content only if there exists an evidential base that can be described independently of the theory, and in relation to which the theory will be more or less adequate. And as with the causal theory, here is where trouble arises.

No matter how rationalistically inclined we are, we would, presumably, agree that the only evidence we have for the existence of an a priori linguistic structure is language as we speak it. We have no more direct access to such a structure than to Kant's twelve categories. But then, it is hard to see how any formulation of that structure can be anything but an hypothesis based on generalizations from speech acts, to be tested by the predictions it allows about future speech acts. For the purposes of a semantic theory, the generalizations must take the form of generalizations about semantic structure, about the relationships that determine the sense of expressions. Again, the evidential base can only be the truth-value we attribute to sentences. The theory captures the a priori structure it relies on only if it fits the evidence.

The intensional theory, like its causal counterpart, is intended to provide an account of reference that is not merely subsidiary to an account of truth. The idea, still, is that an account of meaning and reference is primary. The intensional theory cuts itself off from empirical testability in just the same way as the causal theories do. We can no doubt use a theory of the kind Katz promotes to interpret a language we do not know, once a dictionary is in place, just as we can use a causal theory once the relevant nomological relations have been determined. We cannot, however, use it to construct a dictionary for a language we do not know, which is just another way of saying that there is no way of knowing whether the dictionary we are provided with is a good one or simply legislates the semantics of the language.

A neoclassical theorist might feel we are begging the question against him/her on empiricist assumptions. Katz says:

> The issue between rationalism and empiricism is a question about the structure of the system used for acquiring knowledge. We may picture it as a black box whose input is linguistic information about the use of language and whose output, in the present case, is a semantic description of the language. The question at issue between rationalists and empiricists is, How much of the output is part of the system in its initial state? . . . The output can hardly be used to test these theories if the conception of the output that will be used in framing the test is based on one of them. (Katz, 1979, pp. 109–110)

However, the distinction Katz wants to make here is between reference as ultimately an empirical causal relation and reference as determinable by an account of sense prior to it. He claims, rightly, that we cannot construct a counter-example to the intensional theory of reference that hinges on the assumption that reference is determined by a causal relation: 'there is no way to argue, as Putnam has to argue, from a premise about past references to robot spy devices with the word "cat" to the conclusion that such contraptions constitute the referent of "cat"' (Katz, 1979, p. 110). The present point, however, applies equally to both of these positions, so we can afford to be relatively unconcerned by whatever questions are begged between them. Both intensional and causal theorists proceed on the assumption that there *is* a relation of reference to be elucidated. So in those cases where our intuitions about reference waver, the right theory will settle the question, even if those cases cannot be used to decide the issue between the theories.

From the point of view of Davidson's holistic empirical semantics, there is no issue here. When we do not know what to say about the truth-value of sentences like 'cats never existed', or 'cats are really automatons', the uncertainty is not one that can be eliminated by scrutinizing the relation of reference, by *discovering* to what extent reference is determined by the empirical input and to what extent by the structure of the black box.

It should be clear what common feature of the theoretical endeavours I have discussed blocks the possibility of providing the kind of explanation of language that Davidson is after. In 'Reality Without Reference', Davidson notes that 'the central problem of the philosophy of language' is

> how to explain specifically linguistic concepts like truth (of sentences or utterances), meaning (linguistic), linguistic rule or convention, naming, referring, asserting, and so on — how to analyze some or all of these concepts in terms of concepts of another order. Everything about language can come to seem puzzling, and we would understand it better if we could reduce semantic concepts to others. Or if 'reduce' or 'analyze' are too strong (and I think they are), then let us say, as vaguely as possible, understand semantic concepts in the light of others. (*Inquiries*, p. 219)

For Davidson, semantics is enlightening, as Devitt points out, only in so far as it succeeds in locating a 'place where there is direct contact between linguistic theory and events, actions, or objects described in non-linguistic terms' (*Inquiries*, p. 219). The problem with the theories I have discussed is that they mislocate this place. They are all versions of what Davidson refers to as the building-block theory, in so far as they take the point of empirical contact to be the hooking on to the world of proper names and simple predicates *in the relation of reference*. The idea is then to find a way of describing this relation in non-linguistic terms. The causal theorists hope to do this more or less directly, while intensionalists like Katz want to do it indirectly, by defining type-reference in terms of sense and giving content to sense by linking it to a Chomskyan innate linguistic structure. If either strategy worked, it would, presumably, provide a base for constructing the rest of semantics, including the relation of truth. But both fail, and fail for the same reason, that is, because of their atomistic conception of meaning. The fact that Katz's solution to

Mates's problem rests on his criticism of Frege's building-block metaphor might mislead us into thinking that Katz breaks free from it. But even if the building blocks may be transformed as they combine to produce the meaning of a sentence, Katz still thinks an account of the senses of the atomic constituents of a sentence is primary to an explanation of how they combine to form sentence meanings.

For Davidson, following Quine, this is to go at semantics from the wrong end. If meaning lies in the difference something's being true or false makes, then it is in the attribution of truth-value that the connection to the non-linguistic must be made.

Independently meaningful bits of language are what have empirical impact, and such bits are sentences (or words used as sentences). So it is in sentences being true or false that the connection between semantic concepts and other concepts must be made. But even sentences are not, as Quine made clear, *independently* meaningful in a sense richer than that of being the carriers of truth and falsehood. Sentences are meaningful only embedded in a larger structure, a language. From Davidson's perspective, the problem with both the classical theory and the modern building-block theories is that they represent attempts to make abstractions serve as the explanatory foundations of their own source. That source is the truth-value of sentences.

On the classical conception, there are two parts to the problem of truth: firstly, finding a non-circular way of characterizing reference, and secondly, once the semantical primitives are linked to the world, finding a theory that shows how the truth of sentences depends on the structural relation of their parts. But Davidson's point in 'Reality Without Reference' is that reference is *nothing but* a semantic abstraction. And so the first part of the problem is illusory.[5] Reference cannot be the source of the explanatory import of a theory of truth no matter how we attempt to construe it, because the only way to test any such construal is to trace its effects on the truth value of sentences, that is, to test it against truth.

The argument proceeds from considerations first made clear in 'Truth and Meaning' (*Inquiries*, pp. 17–36). Individual words, says Davidson in this paper, have no meaning at all 'in any sense that transcends the fact that they have a systematic effect on the meanings of the sentences in which they occur' (*Inquiries*, p. 18). We impute meaning to 'each item in the structure [of a sentence] only as an abstraction from the totality of sentences in which it features' (*Inquiries*, p. 22). But then, the only way to give content to the notion that the meaning of a sentence depends upon the meaning of its parts, is to provide a theory that gives the structure of the whole language by abstracting from its potential infinity of sentences the systematic effects on the truth-values of those sentences of the various ways of combining the atomic parts. Contrary to what Katz believes, the principle of compositionality does not require that we must be able to give an account of the senses of words independently of their effect on sentences in order to explain how the meaning of a sentence depends on the meanings of the words in it (see Katz, 1986, p. 83n.).[6]

In a holistic theory of meaning, language as a totality is crucial: "Frege said that only in the context of a sentence does a word have meaning; in the same vein he might have added that only in the context of the language does a sentence and (therefore a word) have meaning" (*Inquiries*, p. 22). The meaning of sentences and words are explained in terms of the role they play in the total structure. The classical approach did not assign any special significance to language as a whole; once we had reference worked out, atomically, so to speak, we could go on to put together sentences, the truth-conditions of which would be worked out on the basis of the references of the parts. On this account, language is an aggregate, and so the structure on which meaning depends is forever beyond its scope. But the causal theory of representation and intensionalist theories of meaning fare no better. They are intended not only to determine *what* the expressions in their domains refer to, but also to explain, in non-semantic terms, *how* it is that they so refer. This explanation is then supposed to explain how it is that sentences have the truth-conditions they do have. But neither kind of theory produces theorems that are testable against evidence available independently of linguistic concepts. Neither hypotheses about causal relations between words (or thought-constituents) and objects nor hypotheses about the nature of innate Chomskyan structures are verifiable without knowledge of the truth-conditions of sentences.

Davidson's proposal is that the semantic conception of truth will provide us with a concept that can be made to serve the function reference was intended to fulfil. While we can never explain the truth-conditions of our sentences in terms of the reference of their constituents, we can use the concept of truth to explain what our words mean. It is obvious that the semantic conception of truth must be very different from the classical understanding, which essentially relies on the concept of reference. 'Reference' is, after all, the concept to be replaced as the touchstone of semantics.

The concept we need is given by a Tarskian theory of truth because it treats words and the structural relations between words as abstractions from the totality of language in just the way Davidson requires. Granting for now that this is a plausible claim – we will try to make more sense of it in chapter 5 – what follows for semantics? It means that we can abandon the attempt to give independent content to semantic terms other than truth. Such concepts are useful only in so far as they 'are posits we need to implement a theory of truth. They serve this purpose without needing independent confirmation or empirical basis' (*Inquiries*, p. 222). The mechanics a theory employs, as well as the ontology it postulates, 'must be treated as so much theoretical construction, to be tested only by its success in predicting the truth-conditions of sentences' (*Inquiries*, p. 74).

There is no independent 'problem of reference' or any other semantic concept – independent, that is, of the construction of a semantic theory of truth. If we can construct a Tarskian theory that succeeds without employing the notion of reference, as Davidson thinks, then the concept simply drops out of empirical semantics. If our theory does make use of the concept, then it is *ipso facto* justified and defined. Going on to explicate reference further in terms of causal connections would then add nothing to our understanding of what it is for words to mean. The attractive simplicity of what we might call Davidson's razor depends on our being able to determine the *success* of a semantic theory without invoking any of the concepts it relies on in our construal of the evidential base. Hence his deconstruction of the idea of reference as a semantically fundamental relation in need of independent definition rests on two conditions. Firstly, we must be able to show that a theory of truth for a language does in fact yield interpretations of its sentences. Secondly, we must be able to construct a theory of truth for a language without relying on other semantic concepts. In other words, we must be able to show that truth indeed is the bridge between non-linguistic and linguistic concepts.

Before going on to a more detailed examination of these demands, I will give a concrete illustration of the fundamental difference between Davidson's empirical semantics and the building-block theories. The question to be addressed is this: if we abandon the concept of reference, do we thereby abandon the idea of a relation between words and objects in the world? The answer will show how Davidson's holistic inversion of semantics redistributes the burden of explanatory weight.

NOTES

1 In Putnam's case, see Putnam (1962, 1975). For Kripke's demolition of the classical view as expressed by Frege and Russell, and those that preserve its spirit by relying on what Kripke calls a cluster concept, see Kripke (1972). From Kripke's perspective, Wittgenstein's concept of family resemblance exemplifies the latter, and so even in his critique of the Fregean notion of reference, Wittgenstein carries the fundamental error with him (see Kripke, 1972, p. 258).

2 Katz discusses this example, first introduced by Putnam (1962). Putnam follows up Donnellan's attack on C. I. Lewis's theory. Wettstein's Smith and Jones argument against intensional theories (for which see Wettstein, 1984) is also handled by the type-reference – token-reference distinction. It is of course only by virtue of Katz's rationalist presupposition that the distinction becomes anything more than a question-begging *ad hoc* manoeuver.

3 Katz suggests that a revised version of Kripke's account of naming might do the trick (Katz, 1979, p. 120). For Kripke's notion of baptism, see Kripke (1972).

4 For Mates's criticism of Frege, see Mates (1952). For Katz's gloss, see Katz (1986, p. 60).

5 As will emerge in the next section, the second part of the problem is equally intractable, unless a concept more general than 'truth' is employed. On Davidson's account, then, the classical problem of truth is doubly insoluble.

6 Davidson, too, subscribes of course to the principle of compositionality, but believes that his holistic explication of it gives content to a truth only vaguely perceived by the classical approach to truth and meaning (see *Inquiries*, for instance pp. 17, 18, 22, 61, 70, 74, 202).

4

Correspondence, Satisfaction and Explanatory Power

Given his pronouncement that nothing makes sentences true (quoted at the end of chapter 2) and remarks along similar lines scattered throughout his papers, it is tempting to read Davidson's semantic conception of truth as a flat rejection of so-called correspondence theories. This interpretation might appear to be supported by Davidson's recent explicit defence of a coherence theory of truth and knowledge (Davidson, 1986b). After all, coherence theories and correspondence theories have traditionally been regarded as incompatible accounts of truth. Furthermore, if a correspondence theory is an attempt to elucidate a relation between language and the world, it would seem to be thoroughly undermined by Davidson's attack on reference, the one concept that would appear to be essential to such a relation.

Yet in 'True to the Facts', Davidson comes out explicitly in favour of the view that some notion of correspondence plays an indispensable role in theories of truth. He writes: 'In this paper I defend a version of the correspondence theory. I think truth can be explained by appeal to a relation between language and the world, and that analysis of that relation yields insight into how, by uttering sentences, we sometimes manage to say what is true' (*Inquiries*, pp. 37–8). What are we to make of this? The least interesting possibility is that Davidson simply changed his mind in the course of the decade and a half that separates his recent defence of a coherence theory from the first publication of 'True to the Facts' in 1969.[1] Fortunately, as a full explanation, this will not do. Davidson introduces his argument for a coherence theory by pointing out that it 'is not in competition with a correspondence theory, but depends for its defense on an argument that purports to show that coherence yields correspondence' (Davidson, 1986b, p. 307).

Is his unwillingness to eschew the idea of correspondence simply a terminological idiosyncrasy on Davidson's part? If we want to say that Davidson is not really a correspondence theorist, we would have to back up this claim by showing that Davidson's reasons for regarding himself as a correspondence theorist are not very good reasons; by showing that the central features of his outline of a theory of meaning would be better served if they were cut free of this notion. This would amount to arguing not that Davidson has changed his view, but that he does not fully perceive the implications of his own position. The assumption here is of course that these 'central features' are features that Davidson himself would regard as in some sense more important than the notion of correspondence. If this assumption were false, we would have no grounds for making claims about what Davidson's views really amount to or what he ought to believe. As it happens, this assumption appears to be true. Davidson employs a concept of correspondence only because it is, in his view, one of the wheels required to keep the theoretical machinery rolling. On the basis of the arguments presented in the previous chapter, I shall assume that Davidson would cheerfully dismiss correspondence the moment he was convinced it was an idle wheel. The point remains, though, that he is not convinced of this, and so there is a strong presumption in favor of taking what he says about correspondence at face value. More strongly, that the theory does employ a notion of correspondence is for Davidson a point in its favour: it means that the theory preserves our realist intuition that truth somehow involves a relation between what we say and the objective features of the world.[2] If we are unable to square these claims with others that he makes, it is just possible that this is due to our inadequate grasp of the latter, rather than an inconsistency on Davidson's part. Taking this possibility seriously is standard hermeneutic procedure, which there is no reason not to follow just because we are studying a paragon of analytical philosophy.

The hermeneutic point I want to make is this: If we understand what function correspondence is intended to fill in the kind of theory Davidson proposes we construct, and if we understand what role the notion is *not* intended to play, we will better be able to see how *un*epistemological Davidson's project really is. We will see that what sets semantic theories of truth apart is not that they give a different account of what truth is from that of classical theories, but that they rely on a different source of conceptual fuel. When we see how Davidson reconciles correspondence and coherence we will see that his is not a semantic theory of truth as much as a truth-based theory of semantics. It will become apparent that Davidson's use of correspondence is not one which commits him to traditional epistemological realism, and that Davidson's own brand of realism is epistemologically and metaphysically innocuous.

In the first part of 'True to the Facts', after arguing against the idea that truth is theoretically redundant, Davidson goes on to rehearse the arguments against traditional correspondence theories. If we try to define correspondence extensionally, there is no preventing the facts to which true sentences correspond from running together into one big fact, so any true sentence corresponds to the fact expressed by itself and any other true statement. This leaves us with an unwieldy ontology of facts and sentences and expressions, and lacks explanatory power. If we go about the matter intensionally, we are no better off: 'Suppose ... we distinguish facts as finely as statements. Of course, not every statement has its fact; only the true ones do. But then, unless we find another way to pick out facts, we cannot hope to explain truth by appeal to them' (*Inquiries*, p. 43). There is nothing surprising in this, once we have been convinced of the chimerical nature of reference, but we are left wondering what Davidson could possibly want from correspondence. The short answer is 'satisfaction'.

Satisfaction is what Tarski actually showed us how to define. A Tarskian definition of truth for a language is derived as a special case from the definition of the relation of satisfaction. In order to get at least a rudimentary grip on this concept and its theoretical significance, we must indulge in a brief excursion into the outskirts of logic.

Why is it not possible to give an extensional definition of truth directly? This would assume an axiomatic base consisting of a finite number of elementary sentences and their truth-conditions, and a recursive clause for each sentential connective, specifying the truth-conditions of composite sentences as a function of the truth-conditions of the atomic sentences and the ways in which they are combined. We would have to make this assumption no matter how we hope to make our theory empirically interesting. It is irrelevant here whether we hope (in vain, it should be unnecessary to add) to explain the truth-conditions of the elementary sentences in terms of an independently defined notion of reference, or whether we want to explain the semantic features of words holistically on the basis of the truth-conditions of the composite sentences. Both approaches founder on their common assumption, which turns out to be insupportable. It is simply not the case that complex sentences are always produced by combining elementary sentences.

If we want a finite specification of how, and from what, sentences are constructed, we are going to get an axiomatic base that yields theorems containing sentences only as a subset of its theorems. The more general constructs of the theorems are both open and closed sentences, in Davidson's terminology, or sentential functions, in Tarski's. A closed sentence, a sentence proper, is a sentential function without open variables. 'x sees y' is a sentential function of the open sentence variety, and it is neither true nor false. 'The leader sees the truth' is of the closed kind, and it is either true or false. But the cost of finitude in axiomatization is that a structural-descriptive theory will only let us get at the latter kind of sentential function *via* the former. As a result, truth does not enter the theoretical picture until we drop the variables from our sentential functions and close our sentences.

As long as we stick to sentential functions generally, what is it that is specified in the theorems? Not truth-conditions, obviously, since only some sentential functions have them. What the theorems give are the conditions of *satisfaction* of particular sentential functions (see Tarski, 1956, p. 193). What satisfies sentential functions are 'functions that map the variables of the object language on to the entities over which they range' (*Inquiries*, p. 47) – according to Davidson, or, in Tarski's terms, infinite sequences (see Tarski, 1956, p. 171).

Infinite sequences are one/many relations where the domain, the 'one', is the free variables of the sentential function, and the counter-domain, the 'many', is a class of ordered n-tuples. In our case, the sentential function 'x sees y' would be satisfied by infinite sequences assigning ordered pairs of entities to the variables x and y just so that each entity assigned to the free variable x sees the entity assigned to y. How do we get to truth from this kind of logical ordering of objects? We saw that 'whether or not a given sequence satisfies a given sentential function depends only on those terms of the sequence which correspond ... with the free variables of the function' (Tarski, 1956, p. 194). It is, in other words, the existence of the free variables that allows us to differentiate between sequences in terms of their relation to sentential functions:

> Thus, in the extreme case, when the function is a [closed] sentence, and so contains no free variable ... the satisfaction of a function by a sequence does not depend on the properties of the terms of the sequence at all. Only two possibilities then remain: either every infinite sequence of classes satisfies a given sentence, or no sequence satisfies it. (Tarski, 1956, p. 194)

A true sentence is satisfied by all sequences and it is therefore an impossible task to distinguish between true sentences on the basis of what 'makes sentences true'.[3] That is, we cannot distinguish between proper sentences in terms of the facts to which they correspond or the sequences by which they are satisfied. Here is where the importance of the concept of satisfaction manifests itself:

> Since different assignments of entities to variables satisfy different open sentences, and since closed sentences are constructed from open, truth is reached, in the semantic approach, by different routes for different sentences. All true sentences end up in the same place, but there are different stories about how they got there. (*Inquiries*, pp. 48–9)

It is 'by running through the recursive account of satisfaction appropriate to the sentence' (*Inquiries*, p. 49), that is, in the proof of the theorems, that a Tarskian theory individuates the truth-conditions of closed sentences. And without such individuation, there would be no hope of empirical testing, since that hope is based precisely on the possibility of differentiating between the truth-conditions assigned to sentences.

We can now see why the classical task of constructing a theory of truth is doubly impossible. Even if there were a way to characterize the relation of reference without relying on other linguistic concepts, thus giving it empirical content, truth would be nowhere in sight. As long as we attempt to get at the truth-predicate directly, and so restrict ourselves to the domain of expressions to which it is applicable, that is, to the domain of closed sentences, we will be unable to axiomatize the systematic effect of our semantic building blocks on the truth-value of the expressions in which they occur. We would be unable, in other words, to give an account of the compositionality of truth-conditions. But, for Davidson, the lesson to be learned is not that correspondence plays no part in a theory of truth. Rather, we must rethink our notion of a *theory* of truth to understand the significance of correspondence.

The concepts of satisfaction and correspondence 'both intend to express a relation between language and the world' (*Inquiries*, p. 48), and so are clearly related. The significance of satisfaction for a Tarskian theory accordingly shows why Davidson refuses to add his name to the lengthening list of philosophers who protest as anachronistic the use of any notion of correspondence in discussions of contemporary truth. But satisfaction is assigned a role in Davidson's theory that is very different from the one traditionally intended for correspondence. The classical attempt is to *explain* truth on the basis of a relation of correspondence; if only we understood correspondence, then we would know what makes sentences true.[4] Here we have returned to the idea of 'the Riddle of Truth' discussed in chapter 2. As we saw, the problem with this idea is that a theory of the nature of truth can never be a source of epistemological justification. No matter how elaborate our attempt at defining correspondence, such a theory remains question-begging; what could we test it against other than what it defines? Elaboration of a relation of correspondence can never confer content on 'truth', just as no theory of reference can ever confer content on 'meaning'. Here the wheels, the connection between the theory and anything that it might hope to explain, are forever disengaged from the engine.

Davidson's strategy is the opposite, reflecting his inversion of the building-block approach. In this theory, correspondence (in the form of satisfaction) derives whatever content it has from the part it plays in a theory which is testable in terms other than its own theoretical constructs. In the theorems produced by the theory we find 'no trace of the notion of correspondence ... no relational predicate that expresses a relation between sentences and what they are about' (*Inquiries*, p. 51). But to conclude from the absence of anything like correspondence in the theorems that no such relation is required by a theory of truth would be an error. In producing its correspondence-free theorems, the theory invokes a relation mapping expressions to objects. And so it does stipulate a relation between words and objects. But in Davidson's theory, this relation is not required to do any epistemological work, and needs no further elaboration or justification. As a postulate of the theory, it is defined through the empirical content of the theory, derived from the theorems.

To suppose that a relation between words and objects is in need of independent construal in terms of, say, reference, is to conceive of this relation as the source of the empirical content of a theory of truth. And we would conceive of it this way only if we thought we needed correspondence to determine the truth-value of sentences. But there is no way to somehow confront sentences with something non-linguistic in order to see whether they are true. Realizing this has led many philosophers to dismiss the notion of correspondence altogether. This, however, is too hasty. Certainly correspondence is epistemologically useless, but it is semantically necessary. The concept of satisfaction enables us to give a theoretical determination of not the truth-value but the truth-conditions of sentences: To know what it is for 'snow is white' to be true is to know something that is captured by a theory of truth for English. Since that theory works by mapping words and objects in a certain way, we have, Davidson argues, all the justification we need for invoking a relation of correspondence. But the further question of *whether* 'snow is white' is true cannot be answered in terms of this relation. Epistemological justification is a matter of coherence. Only other sentences can be *evidence* for the truth of a sentence.

Nevertheless, Davidson himself is inclined to say that his theoretical use of truth and correspondence makes him a realist. Dummett, for one, agrees, and in 'What is a Theory of Meaning?' (Dummett, 1975) and 'What is a Theory of Meaning? (II)'

(Dummett, 1976), he levels a forceful attack precisely against what he sees as the realist presuppositions of Davidson's semantics.[5] Opposing his own molecular, verificationist – or falsificationist – account of language to Davidson's truth-based holism, Dummett says:

> What differentiates such a theory from one in which truth is the central notion is, first, that meaning is not directly given in terms of the condition for a sentence to be true, but for it to be verified; and, secondly, that the notion of truth, when it is introduced, must be explained, in some manner, in terms of our capacity to recognize statements as true, and not in terms of a condition which transcends human capacities. (Dummett, 1976, p. 116)

For Dummett, that truth is an experience-transcendent concept is fatal to any semantics which is designed, like Davidson's, to employ 'truth' as its core concept. The reason is that

> where we are concerned with a representation in terms of propositional knowledge of some practical ability, and, in particular, where that practical ability is the mastery of a language, it is incumbent upon us, if our account is to be explanatory, not only to specify what someone has to know for him to have that ability, but also what it is for him to have that knowledge, that is, what we are taking as constituting a manifestation of a knowledge of those propositions; if we fail to do this, then the connection will not be made between the theoretical representation and the practical ability it is intended to represent. (Dummett, 1976, p. 121)

The problem, then, for Dummett, is that there can be no manifestation of the required kind of the knowledge of truth-conditions in cases where it is 'in principle impossible to know the truth of some true statement' (Dummett, 1976, p. 99). Hence, Dummett argues, we should explicate meaning in terms of grounds for assertion rather than truth, and we should give up the law of bivalence for those statements the truth-value of which is in principle undecidable, which is to say that we should be non-realists about classes of statements of this kind.

Dummett's anti-realism was recently challenged head on by Anthony Appiah, in a book called *For Truth in Semantics* (Appiah, 1986). Appiah, like Dummett, believes that issues like the one between realists and anti-realists can be resolved by paying careful attention to semantics. He aims to show that Dummett is wrong, and that we ought to be realists about, for instance, statements concerning in-principle inaccessible regions of space-time.

Now this debate has endured, in only slightly different garb, for centuries, and it is not my intention to contribute to it here. The present point is that on my reading, Davidson is not a party to it, Dummett's polemic notwithstanding.

The issue between Dummett and Appiah turns on what to do about the alleged lag between assertibility-conditions and truth-conditions. The anti-realist wants to get rid of it by suggesting that certain sentences − those sentences the truth-value of which might elude us even if we had all the evidence in the world − are not, like other sentences, either true or false. The realist wants to keep the gap open as a receptacle for metaphysical filler, a space which provides room for things to be what they independently are, or some such notion.

The notion of truth operative in Davidson's work, however, is not the kind required by realist metaphysicians. A true statement for Davidson is simply one we would assert when all the evidence is in. No statement is ever indefeasible, but that is, firstly, for the epistemic reason that we never possess *all* the evidence there might be − and *not* because of a potential discrepancy between all possible evidence and the way things really are − and, secondly, for the semantic, Quinian reason that it is always possible to play around with the truth-value of sentences in a theory while preserving the empirical content of the theory as a whole.

To make the debate between realists and anti-realists hinge on the law of bivalence in semantics, Dummett must make a hard − and unsupported − distinction between statements that are in principle verifiable and those that are not, and between direct and indirect evidence for the truth of a statement. But these epistemological distinctions are suspect, to say the least. What, for instance, is the difference between an in-principle unverifiable sentence and a practically unverifiable sentence? Why are statements about inaccessible regions of space-time unverifiable in principle, rather than practically unverifiable? Are there a priori arguments that show the impossibility of time travel? If, say, some global physical event caused a glitch in our genes that deafened our offspring and eventually the entire species, would statements about how things sound a couple of generations down the line become in principle unverifiable? To suggest that a sentence may be false in spite of the indications of all available evidence is uncontroversial. But to suggest that a sentence might be false in spite of the indications of all *possible* evidence, or that it may be true or false even though no evidence either way is conceivable, is to introduce a metaphysically laden concept of truth that carries a much heavier burden than Davidson's concept of truth is asked to do.

The relation of correspondence that Davidson endorses is one where the *relata* are epistemically on a par. It is a relation of correspondence between observed utterances and specifiable features of the environment (in the broadest possible sense). The realism here is not of a kind that carries metaphysical significance, since neither of the *relata* can serve as an underpinning of the other. It is, rather, a reminder that we can be no more, or less, sure about meanings than about facts in the world. Davidson's realism comes to this: If we think we understand what people say, we must also regard most of our observations about the world we live in as correct. Davidson does not provide metaphysical assurance of our connection with reality, he simply makes the point that if we try to give up the world, we must also give up language.

Davidson's reconciliation of correspondence and coherence is summed up in the slogan 'correspondence without confrontation' (Davidson, 1986b, p. 307). It hinges on a clear grasp of the distinction between semantics and epistemology. Davidson proclaims himself a realist because the only way to construct a semantic theory of truth, to give the truth-conditions of sentences, is to postulate a relation between language and the world. But this relation does not serve justificatory purposes of any kind.[6] He is a coherentist because the only way to test claims to truth, to determine the truth-value of sentences, is to see how they cohere with other truths. If we miss the first point, we stand in danger not of losing touch with the world but of opening up the metaphysical space where the epistemological brands (albeit dressed up in semantic disguises) of realism and anti-realism confront one another. Davidson's realism is realistic only in the negative sense that his naturalist semantics leaves no room for idealism. Missing the second point, that epistemic justification is a matter of coherence, we remain bogged down in the hopeless search for the link between the world and our representations of it, the search for the special mark of truth that would justify our beliefs.

NOTES

1 In *The Journal of Philosophy*, 66, 1969, pp. 748–64.

2 In a review of *Inquiries* (Hacking, 1984), Ian Hacking says:

> In conjecturing a theory of truth about the speech of another person, we must ... arrange for him a coherent bundle of beliefs and utterances, coherent by our lights, the only lights we have. But what we call reality is not something that can be identified independently of how we identify it. Hence that which we, by using the standard of coherence, call true, unsurprisingly, and vacuously, 'corresponds' to the world. (Hacking, 1984, p. 57)

This appears to me to obscure the fundamental point that for Davidson coherence and correspondence are categorically different notions, in that the former is epistemological and the latter semantic.

3 For Davidson's account of this argument, see *Inquiries* (p. 48).

4 Davidson is not the first to reject an epistemological explication of truth on the grounds that it is a transparent concept. In one of the letters to Mersenne (16 October 1639), contrasting Lord Herbert of Cherbury's approach in *De Veritate* with his own, Descartes remarks: 'He examines what truth is; I have never thought of doing so, because it seems a notion so transcendentally clear that nobody can be ignorant of it' (Descartes, 1639).

5 These essays, which take the form of a polemic against Davidson's position, comprise only a small part of Dummett's ground-breaking work in semantics. For an incisive attempt to pin down the nature of the tangled disagreement between Davidson and Dummett, see Akeel Bilgrami's paper 'Meaning, Holism and Use' (1986).

6 This appears to be Rorty's point in 'Pragmatism, Davidson and Truth' (1986). Rorty also claims that this does not leave much content to the designation 'realist', and wants to enlist Davidson in the pragmatists' attempt to dissolve metaphysical questions, a 'struggle [that] is *beyond* realism and anti-realism' (Rorty, 1986, p. 354).

5

Convention T

It should be no surprise that in Davidson's eyes the chief virtue of Tarski's work is in providing a method of defining truth for a language without depending on some property or relation that makes sentences true. Tarski's construal of truth does not rely on a relation to be explained. In so far as a relation is involved, it is as an explication of the property of truth, which derives its conceptual content not from a relation but from an extensional definition. But if this virtue of a Tarskian theory is one it possesses because it applies to a *formalized* language, then of what use can it be to Davidson?

In order to give a definition of truth for a language, a full characterization of the truth predicate in terms of the axioms and rules of inference of the theory, Tarski relies on a metalanguage with significantly stronger ontological resources than those available in the object language. For formalized languages, this is an unproblematic move. But in the case of a natural language, it cannot be made. This becomes immediately apparent when we imagine a case 'where a significant fragment of a language (plus one or two semantical predicates) is used to state its own theory of truth' (*Inquiries*, p. 132). As speakers of English, we do not have available an ontologically stronger metalanguage in which to state our theory of truth for English. Any attempt to construct an ontologically more resourceful metalanguage would be self-defeating, since success would simply represent an expansion of our natural language, which is also the object language. Natural languages are forever unfinished, and so we cannot 'specify structurally those expressions of language which we call sentences, still less can we distinguish among them [on the basis of their structure] the true ones' (Tarski, 1956, p. 164).

The feature of natural languages that Tarski refers to as their universality also gives rise to antinomies of self-reference like the paradox of the liar. Consistency is the price paid for the capacity of natural languages to absorb anything they touch, and it is precisely this capacity that distinguishes them from formalized languages. So, Tarski concludes, 'the very possibility of a consistent use of the expression "true sentence" which is in harmony with the laws of logic and the spirit of everyday language seems to be very questionable, and consequently the same doubt attaches to the possibility of constructing a correct definition of this expression' (Tarski, 1956, p. 165). Davidson is of course interested in the question of meaning for natural languages. But how can this question be solved by way of Tarskian theories of truth, when Tarski's method of defining the truth predicate for a language relies essentially on the additional ontological wealth of the language of the theory relative to the object language? As we have seen, Tarski himself takes this difference in available entities to imply the exclusion of natural languages from the domain of applicability of the theory he demonstrates. If he were right, it would appear that the scope of Tarskian theories is limited in such a way that Davidson's purpose would be defeated.

Whether natural languages will yield to the formalization required for the application of Tarskian theories of truth is a question upon which Davidson's project pivots. Throughout Davidson's writings on the topic he admonishes against the kind of pessimism displayed both by the father of the theory and contemporary critics alike (see for instance *Inquiries*, pp. 27–9, 58–9, 70–1) To some extent, the matter is one of faith. But not in a sense different from that involved in pursuing any research programme; it is a matter for reasoned, even if not conclusive, judgement based on empirical investigations.

To the claim that we cannot give an explicit definition of truth for a natural language along the lines drawn by Tarski, Davidson responds that this is indeed the case, and fortunately we can get by without one. We can, he says 'require no more than a *theory* of truth; to go beyond to an explicit definition does widen the gap between the resources of the object language and of the metalanguage' (*Inquiries*, p. 72). If we settle for a recursive characterization of the truth-predicate of, say, English, we need invoke no entities to state our theory that are not available in English, or immediately upon postulation absorbed into English. But even if a recursive characterization of the truth predicate requires no ontological propagation outside the object language, it does require what Davidson refers to as an 'increase in ideology' even if this increase 'can be limited to the semantic concepts' (*Inquiries*, p. 72). This means that while we need not postulate *entities* like sets, classes or sequences or, for that matter, propositions, that are exclusive to the metalanguage in order to get our theory going, we do need to invoke certain *concepts* thus restricted, in particular, the truth-predicate itself. But this is no catastrophe. It implies only that when we are constructing an explicit truth-theory for a language, we are expanding the language, actually or potentially. We are actually expanding it if the language of the theory is also the object language, and so ensuring the continuous emergence of domains for further theory construction, which is another way of saying that a language can never complete its own truth-theory, because in treating itself both as object and meta-language it is always stretching its conceptual resources. We are potentially expanding the language if it is a language different from the one in which the theory is stated. Rather than saying, as Davidson does, that 'there may in the nature of the case always be something we grasp in understanding the language of another (the concept of truth) that we cannot communicate to him' (*Inquiries*, p. 29), we could better express this idea by suggesting not that we cannot communicate what we have grasped, but that in so far as we do succeed in communicating our understanding it ensures its own incompleteness by forcing the conceptual or ideological expansion of the object language. By settling for this kind of incompleteness, we capture what is intuitively convincing in the idea of the universality of natural languages (that there cannot be a domain of language somehow beyond and in principle inaccessible to a natural language), without prejudging the question of the possibility of constructing a theory of truth for a natural language.

Once we give up the attempt to settle it on a priori grounds, this question becomes more interesting. It also becomes much harder to dismiss Davidson's project. This is because he is not setting forth a specific empirical hypothesis, a theory of meaning subject to testing; he is rather giving the measure of such hypotheses, specifying the requirements a theory might reasonably be expected to meet, suggesting that they would be met by candidates embodying a structure of a certain kind. But Davidson is not wedded to any particular candidate. He is wedded to the quasi-empirical claim that we would not, as he puts it in a response to one of Tarski's remarks on the prospect, 'have to reform a natural language out of all recognition before we could apply formal semantic methods' (*Inquiries*, p. 29). This makes the matter one of degree, and so it suffices for Davidson, in justifying his approach, to point out that significant progress has been made in establishing methods for formalizing important fragments of natural languages. Particular setbacks or difficulties must always be weighed against overall progress and the general merits of the strategy, namely the elucidation of meaning without 'meanings', entities which have so far proved to be obfuscatory rather than clarifying, and a sharpening of the foci of the empirical study of language (see for instance *Inquiries*, pp. 21, 60).

The fundamental objection to Davidson's suggestion rests, as we have seen, on the assumption that natural and formalized languages are different in kind. If this were true, it would be impossible to elucidate one in terms of the other: in formalizing a natural language we would lose precisely those features semantic theory purports to investigate. Not unexpectedly, Davidson takes issue with this assumption:

> The contrast [between natural and formal languages] is better drawn in terms of guiding interests. We can ask for a description of the structure of a natural language: the answer must be an empirical theory, open to test and subject to error, and doomed to be to some extent incomplete and schematic. Or we can ask about the formal properties of the structures we thus abstract. The difference is like that between pure and applied geometry. (*Inquiries*, pp. 59–60)

Subjecting a (fragment of a) natural language to formalization and giving its structure with a Tarskian theory of truth, is, Davidson implies, useful for certain purposes, specifically for the purposes of giving accounts of truth and meaning. There are many purposes for which it would not be useful, purposes, for instance, for which the diachronic aspect of language is essential. If we are interested in the nature of the structures themselves, we can treat our abstracted formalizations as atemporal and delineated, that is, as formalized languages yielding to complete theoretical descriptions; if we are interested in understanding a natural language, we must regard our abstractions as incomplete and without permanently fixed delineations, with the consequences this has for the status of our truth-theory, namely, that it cannot be developed into a complete definition.

Construing the relationship between natural and formalized languages this way, Davidson undercuts objections to the viability of his project raised on a priori grounds. For Davidson and everyone else, it remains to be seen whether we are able to formalize a natural language (or a significant fragment) in such a way that the characterization of the truth-predicate is supported by our intuitions of its extension. As Davidson remarks, 'here the proof of the pudding will certainly be in the proof of the right theorems' (*Inquiries*, p. 28).

It is worth noting, however, that the possibility of giving a theoretical description of linguistic competence by way of a formalization of language now becomes linked to the relative importance to communication of the abstracted synchronic aspects of language on the one hand and the diachronic or dynamic aspects on the other. I shall argue in chapter 8 that it is this latter issue which finally leads Davidson to conclude that we cannot make theoretical sense of the concept of a language.

Presently, however, I turn to Davidson's appropriation of Tarski's formal model, and its application to natural-language semantics. This will provide an answer to the key question, how can the truth-conditions of sentences be said to give their meanings?

As we have seen, that there is no hope of attaining an explicit definition of truth for a natural language is no reason to abandon Tarski's method. Its promise lies in the fact that whatever the logical and ontological resources the theory uses, it produces theorems which state the truth-conditions for the sentences of the object language by giving the translations of those sentences in the metalanguage. This means that no resources not available in the object language are needed to see that the theorems are true, as long as we take for granted the correctness of the translation. Tarski's theory succeeds in defining truth for a delineated object language, as opposed to arbitrarily stipulating the extension of the truth-predicate, precisely because the theorems it generates are trivial. Were they not, we would have no way of knowing that the theory indeed gave the right extension of the truth predicate for our object language. And they are trivial only because Tarski stipulates that we must know what it is for a sentence of the object language to 'have the same meaning' as a sentence in the metalanguage.

In formalized languages, the theorems are recognized by their syntax alone. This 'syntactical test is merely meant to formalize the relation of synonymy or translation, and this relation is taken for granted in Tarski's work on truth' (*Inquiries*, p. 150). In other words, Tarski succeeds in giving a definition of truth by relying on a concept of translation. But, for Davidson, the point is to explain what it is for words to mean; what he is after is just what Tarski leaves unanalysed. So he turns Tarski on his head: 'Our outlook inverts Tarski's: we want to achieve an understanding of meaning or translation by assuming a prior grasp of truth' (*Inquiries*, p. 150). This, Davidson believes, will provide us with a way of judging the acceptability of the theorems of a theory 'that is not syntactical, and makes no use of the concepts of translation, meaning, or synonymy, but is such that acceptable . . . [theorems] . . . will in fact yield interpretations' (*Inquiries*, p. 150). The fact that no such theory of interpretation for a natural language will ever be either complete or wholly consistent, Davidson sees as a reflection not of the inadequacy of his semantic approach, but of the nature of natural languages.

How can the theorems of a truth-theory be expected to give us interpretations of sentences? This is to ask how a truth-theory can satisfy Davidson's first requirement of a theory of meaning. For an answer we must look more closely at the kind of theory Tarski developed.

The theorems of such a theory are of course the famous T-sentences. Tarski's T-sentences are biconditionals of the form

$$\text{`}s \text{ is true if and only if } p\text{'}$$

Here *s* stands for what is called a canonical description of a sentence in the object language of the theory (that is, *s* mentions the sentence); *p* stands for the sentence itself (if the object language is contained by the metalanguage) or its translation into the metalanguage (if the languages are different); 'is true' is the place holder for the truth-predicate (see *Inquiries*, p. 66). As Davidson points out, it is easy to be misled by the triviality of these biconditionals; one feels that sentences about the colour of snow and cats on mats take us little distance towards an understanding of the nature of truth. This is correct, in the sense that T-sentences are not epistemologically informative. But this should not surprise us, since the issue here is the property of truth, not the question of how we determine the truth-values of sentences. If we are surprised, it is either because we are really concerned with the latter issue, or because we are guilty of the epistemological confusion described in chapters 2 and 4, thinking that knowing how to establish the truth-conditions of a sentence will tell us how to pin down its truth-value. As long as we muddle those two questions together and look for that special property which 'apartheid is a moral abomination', 'outbursts of xenophobia can usually be correlated with economic decline' and '*la neige est blanche*' all have in common and which *makes* them all true, then talk of T-sentences will leave us mystified.

However, to be thus dismissive of T-sentences is to completely miss their point, which is that

> since there is a T-sentence corresponding to each sentence of the language for which truth is in question, the totality of T-sentences exactly fixes the extension, among the sentences, of any predicate that plays the role of the words 'is true' ... [hence] ... any predicate is a truth predicate that makes all T-sentences true. (*Inquiries*, p. 65)

Accordingly, a finite set of axioms and procedural rules (logical axioms) that entails a true T-sentence for every possible truth functional sentence of a language, is a theory of truth for that language.[1] Such a theory obeys convention T, Tarski's celebrated criterion of adequacy for theories of truth.[2]

At first blush, convention T appears to be circular. How can Tarski test the adequacy of a theory of truth by appealing to the notion of true T-sentences? Part of the answer is that when a theory determines the extension of the truth-predicate for a given language, that language, by definition, does not include the T-sentences as expressions. So when we ask whether the T-sentences are true, we are asking whether they belong to a set of expressions denoted by a predicate other than the one defined by the theory. As long as we retain a firm grip on the notions of metalanguage and object language, and the truth predicate as a predicate defined for a language, there is no danger of circularity. But somehow this answer does not seem to completely reassure us.[3] The question remains of what exactly it is a Tarskian theory tells us.

A theory satisfying convention T answers the question of what we *mean* by calling a sentence of a language L true by showing how the corresponding T-sentence of meta-L follows as a theorem from a determinate set of axioms. In other words, to know the theory, and to know that it is a truth-theory, is to know what it is for any arbitrary sentence of L to be true — as distinct from knowing whether an arbitrary sentence of L is true. To know whether the theory is a *good* theory, we must possess what Davidson calls 'a preanalytic understanding of truth', which is to say that we must know how to apply the truth-predicate of the metalanguage — though knowing how to apply a concept does not, of course, imply that we can give an explicit definition of it. But if the theory *is* a good theory, then knowing it, and knowing it to be a truth-theory, suffices for our understanding the truth-predicate of the language L. In *assessing* the theory, what we are asking is whether it is indeed true that the truth conditions for a given sentence are what the theorems of the theory state them to be. More simply, we ask whether ringing the changes on the theory consistently gives us true T-sentences. It is clear that we cannot answer this question if we have no conception of truth independently of the definition provided by our theory.

We must not, however, draw the hasty conclusion that a Tarskian theory is circular or question-begging. It is true that if all we are offered is a bunch of sentences of the form '*s* is true if and only if *p*', we are told nothing — neither epistemically nor semantically — that we do not already know. To tell whether the bunch consists of true T-sentences, we would have to know everything about the truth-predicate of L that the 'theory' purports to tell us. But convention T requires that *p* be a *translation* of the sentence named by *s*. So if we understand what it is for a sentence of L to mean the same thing as a sentence of the metalanguage, we would be able to assess the T-sentences without an independent understanding of the truth-predicate of the object language L.

When judging the adequacy of a theory of truth for a formalized language, some pre-theoretical understanding is certainly required. It is this pre-theoretical grasp that allows us to see the T-sentences as trivial or trivially true. And it is only because we are able to so see them that we can read them as confirming instances of our theory. But as we saw, this understanding is not an understanding of the truth-predicate of L, the concept defined by the theory, so it is not question-begging. Because of the translation requirement, we can assess the T-sentences without knowing in advance what it is for a sentence of the object language to be true. For Tarski, the pre-theoretical understanding required in testing a theory should not be expressed as an understanding of *truth*. A good or adequate theory is one which gives adequate T-sentences as theorems, and adequacy is cashed in by Tarski in terms of sameness of meaning. Translation of one formalized language into another (that may or may not contain the object language) is simply a matter of logical legislation, which is why Tarski can leave the notion of translation primitive without loss of conceptual content.[4] Sameness of meaning is just the coextension of expressions, and the extension of an expression is stipulated by its form. Hence, the adequacy of T-sentences in formalized languages is determined by syntactical form alone.

We have still not been given any epistemological news, but we have been told something semantically informative about the truth-predicate of the object language, namely, that it applies to all and only those sentences the translations of which we would assert. In terms of natural languages, this does not seem to amount to much, but that is partly because we find it difficult to hold on to the notion of true-in-a-language when we think of, say, English and German. We have a vague suspicion that understanding what it is for two sentences of different languages to mean the same thing just *is* to have a pre-analytical grasp of truth. If '*der Schnee ist weiß*' and 'snow is white' mean the same thing, is this not just because they are truth-functionally equivalent? But with this muddled question – it does not require much reflection to see that 'truth-functional equivalence' and 'sameness of meaning' are neither truth-functionally equivalent nor synonymous – we are not objecting to Tarski. We are, rather, conceding a point on which Davidson trades: truth and meaning are not independently definable.

There is another reason why we might feel cheated by Tarski. We have been discussing the meta-theoretical question of how we know when a theory of truth is correct. The unproblematic distinction (that is, the clear and unambiguous logical relation) between truth and meaning, on which Tarski relies in his demonstration of a way to define truth for a formalized language, seems specious in the context of natural languages. Here we are not sure what it would be to leave meaning primitive and define truth by means of it without begging the question of truth. This is fine by Tarski, as well as by Davidson. Tarski, after all, despaired of defining truth for natural languages. And meaning is the last concept that Davidson would want to leave primitive. What is not fine is that our unease with the meta-question might blind us to the different question of what a correct theory of truth for a language actually would tell us.

If we are exclusively concerned with how to determine whether a theory of truth for German in English is a good theory, the seeming uninformativeness of the T-sentences might block our view of the fact that the importance of the theorems does not lie in the theorems themselves, but in their derivation. The power of a Tarskian theory lies in its showing how we can get, from a finite stock of primitive building blocks and logical (recursive) axioms, all and only the true T-sentences for a language. Or more precisely, we should say that its power lies in showing how we can get from all and only the true T-sentences of a language to a finite stock of words and operators, each with a specific function.

The theory is a description of the logical structure of the language. So even if the verification of a theory of truth for German does presuppose that we already have a concept of truth, the theory would still be rich in content. At the price of leaving truth primitive, it explains everything we need to know to understand German speakers. It explains this because, in producing those trivial T-sentences, it makes explicit how the truth-conditions of the sentences of German depend upon the building blocks from which they are constructed and the ways in which those blocks are put together. It is by forcing the theoretical recovery of this structure that the restrictions imposed by convention T pay their way, not by providing a list of T-sentences.

As we have seen, Tarski employs the concept of translation in his formulation of convention T. As we have also seen, this will not do for Davidson's purposes. In Davidson's version (in one of them, anyway) convention T goes like this:

> A theory of truth will be materially adequate, that is, will correctly determine the extension of the truth-predicate, provided it entails, for each sentence s of the object language, a theorem of the form 's it true if and only if p' where 's' is replaced by a description of s and 'p' is replaced by a sentence that is true if and only if s is. (*Inquiries*, p. 150)

This formulation substitutes the truth equivalence of s and p for Tarski's stipulation of p as an interpretation of s. But if truth equivalence is all that is required, how can we expect the constraints of convention T to capture theories that yield interpretations as theorems? We do want p to be an interpretation of s; that is precisely the point. But we want this to come about as a result of requirements formulated without making use of 'interpretation' or notions of that ilk. And now it looks as if sentences like, '"snow is white" is true if and only if grass is green' are perfectly good T-sentences. They are, too, and T-sentences like this one serve to remind us of the hopelessness of the task of distinguishing sentences on the basis of some extensionally construed relation of correspondence (see *Inquiries*, p. 25). But as we saw in chapter 4, this should not inspire us to attempt an intensional construal. If we are discouraged at this point, it is only because we are again looking too hard at the theorems themselves, rather than at the theory that generates them. The theory has to produce the T-sentence for, in this case 'snow is white', on the basis of the structure of this sentence. The T-sentence must fall out deductively as we, starting with the theoretical primitives, run through the recursions to the truth-conditions of the sentence via the satisfaction of the sentential function of which it is a special case (see *Inquiries* pp. 48–9, 61). It is because the theory must reach the truth-conditions of 'snow is white' *and every other sentence of the language* in this way, using the same finite resources to account for any of an infinity of possible sentences, that we can expect the right side of the biconditional to be an interpretation of the left. Then, as Davidson says (referring to the T-sentence linking 'snow is white' to the colour of grass as '(S)':

> The grotesqueness of (S) is in itself nothing against a theory of which it is a consequence, provided the theory gives the correct results for every sentence (on the basis of structure, there being no other way). It is not easy to see how (S) could be party to such an enterprise, but if it were − if, that is, (S) followed from a characterization of the predicate 'is true' that led to the invariable pairing of truths with truths and falsehoods with falsehoods − then there would not, I think, be anything essential to the idea of meaning that remained to be captured. (*Inquiries*, p. 26)

In short, Davidson believes, the difficulty we have in imagining what it would *mean* for 'snow is white' to mean 'grass is green' is exactly the difficulty we have in coming up with a theory which yields (S) − coming up with a theory that yields (S) and satisfies convention T, that is, because by now it should be clear that it is the holistic constraint imposed by convention T that is the key to the connection between truth and meaning. Each theorem tells us very little, since only a pairing of truth values is required. But this should not mislead us into giving up on an extensional account of meaning: 'The present thought is rather to expect to find a minimum of information about the correctness of the theory at each single point; it is the potential infinity of points that makes the difference' (*Inquiries*, p. 225)[5]

The idea that the truth of the theorems suffices to ensure that a theory of truth captures the meaning of the expressions of a language has met much resistance. In the editors' introduction to *Truth and Meaning* (Evans and McDowell, 1976), Gareth Evans and John McDowell echo the contributions to that volume of J. A. Foster (1976) and Brian Loar (1976):

> The fact that each axiom of a truth theory has its impact upon an infinite number of T-sentences does indeed have the consequence that it is difficult for counterfeit theories to pass the test provided

by [convention T]. But . . . it is not impossible. Axioms for individual expressions may be chosen which, even though they disperse their inaccuracy, if construed as giving the meanings of those expressions, over as many T-sentences as there are sentences in which the expressions occur, nevertheless preserve the truth of all the T-sentences . . . It is thus obvious that more stringent conditions must be imposed upon a theory of truth, if it is to serve as a theory of meaning, than that its T-sentences be true. (Evans and McDowell, 1976, p. xiv)

It is always possible, given any one theory of truth, to derive from it, with the aid of simple logical devices, a second theory that extensionally matches the first, yet would be intuitively unacceptable as a theory of meaning. Evans and McDowell conclude from this that if a theory of truth for a language is to serve as a theory of meaning, it must also be constrained by conditions the formulation of which 'would involve employing psychological concepts' (Evans and McDowell, 1976, p. xv).

In my view, this conclusion is mistaken. Rather than introducing psychological concepts as primitives in semantics, we should recall that a natural language is never a complete, clearly delineated entity, and hence give up the idea that a language can ever be modelled by a completed truth-theory. For it is only on the assumption that there is some one theory or other that definitively captures the meaning of the words of a language, that we can imagine a situation where convention T could not be used to rule out a 'counterfeit theory'. If we give up the requirement that the formulation of a theory of truth for a language must at some point be complete, we will never be in this bind. For while it is true that, at any one point, we can always derive a counterfeit theory from the theory we are presently working with, there is no reason in principle why we cannot carry on our theory construction in precisely such a way that convention T will exclude one of the theories. The theory we then arrive at will be different from either of the first two, in that it is based on new empirical evidence, and again it will be possible to derive a counterfeit theory. But, again, we can expand our empirical evidence in such a way that the theories are brought into conflict in a manner which allows us to discriminate between them on the basis of convention T alone. We are stuck in the unacceptable position that concerns Evans and McDowell only if at some point in our theory construction we decide that we are finished, or if we somehow run out of empirical evidence. But this will not happen, since the number of possible sentences of a language is infinite.

Towards the end of chapter 6 I shall return to this point, which is disregarded by those who deem it necessary to impose psychological or other constraints on theories of truth in order to produce theories of meaning. I will then show how the incompletable process of theory construction serves to eliminate the kind of counterfeit theories that worry Foster, Loar, Evans and McDowell, without the need to rely on criteria other than truth.

For now, we can conclude not that the stuff of meaning is not extensional, but that we need an unending supply of it. In this potentially infinite mapping of sentences and their truth-conditions, the theory assigns specific structural roles to its finite resources. That is to say, it assigns meanings to words and defines the logical operations by abstracting their role in determining the truth-conditions of sentences. The theory captures the impact of a sentence being true or false on the language as a whole, because it reflects this in the structural role it assigns to the terms of that sentence. A theorem accordingly gives the meaning of a sentence in the sense of 'assigning the sentence a semantic location in the pattern of sentences that comprise the language' (*Inquiries*, p. 225). And we need no other sense in which to ascribe meaning to a sentence. So a structural theory of truth for a language of this kind just *is* an interpretation of that language. But it is the *right* interpretation only if it assigns *correct* truth-conditions to the sentences of the language, that is, if its theorems are true. But how do we know this? Even if we have no trouble applying the truth-predicate of the language of the theory — and so possess the required pre-theoretical understanding — how do we know that a theory invariably matches truths with truths and falsehoods with falsehoods without already knowing the meaning of the sentences of the language we are giving the theory for? What we are asking now is how a Tarskian theory satisfies Davidson's second requirement of a theory of meaning. We want to know how it can be tested, that is, how we can use the concept of truth as a source of empirical content.

NOTES

1 Strictly speaking, an infinite number of axioms might also be said to constitute a truth-theory. But without the restriction of finitude, 'a theory would yield no insight into the structure of the language and would provide no hint of an answer to the question how the meaning of a sentence depends on its composition' (*Inquiries*, p. 56). We would for instance not be able to rule out a theory which gives the extension of a truth-predicate for a language simply by taking all true T-sentences of the language as its axioms.

2 For Tarski's formulation of convention T, see Tarski (1956, pp. 187–8.)

3 It does not reassure us, because our intuitive concept of truth is absolute. What this means will be explored in chapter 6, where the fundamental significance of a concept of absolute truth for Davidson's theory will emerge.

4 Davidson says: 'Since Tarski was interested in defining truth, and was working with artificial languages where stipulation can replace illumination, he could take the concept of translation for granted' (*Inquiries*, p. 172). Compare his remark that 'the notion of translation, which can be made precise for artificial languages on which interpretations are imposed by fiat, has no precise or even clear application to natural languages' (*Inquiries*, p. 204).

5 Compare the following remark: 'The desired effect is to extract a rich concept ... from thin bits of evidence ... by imposing a formal structure on enough bits' (*Inquiries*, p. 74).

6
Radical interpretation (I): The principle of charity

In constructing a truth-theory for a natural language we attempt to capture the structure of something which is in an important sense given. We attempt to produce a theory on which every sentence of the language in question is matched by a coextensional sentence of the language of the theory. If we are playing with formal models, concerned only with the reproduction of structures, this is not an achievement to be proud of; we simply legislate. In this case, either the extension of the sentences of the object language or the extension of the sentences of a model of it are defined by the theory. Natural languages, on the other hand, constrain us at both ends. Sentences of natural languages, unlike those of constructed models, already have an extension. This double constraint is what allows empirical questions to be framed. Whether the theorems capture co-extension can only be an issue if both the object language and the language of the theory can be given independently of each other.

How do we know whether our theorems capture co-extension? To ask this question is to ask for the empirical content of a theory of truth. We cannot, of course, simply look and see whether the theorems of a given theory are true, just as there is no way to look and see if $e = mc^2$ is true. Like $e = mc^2$, the theorems, the T-sentences, must be nomological — that is, they must be able to support counter-factuals and subjunctives, and they must be confirmed by their concrete instances but not confined to them. Knowing the theory without knowing that it is a theory, without knowing, specifically, that its theorems are law-like we would be left uncomprehending in the face of any concrete speech act (see *Inquiries*, pp. 26n., 173–5)

To get a clear idea of what we do look at, and how what we look at supports our theory, we imagine a situation where we are attempting to translate into our own language one that is completely new to us and unrelated to anything we have ever heard of, spoken by a group of people about whom we know nothing. Here the task of radical interpretation is crystallized.[1]

The interpreter in this situation has nothing to go on but what she sees the native speakers do and the sounds she hears them utter.[2] Looking for causal relations between the speakers' words and objects in their world would be like looking for a drop of water in the sea. The interpreter would have no way even to pick out individual words, except in so far as they get used as sentences, such as when '*gavagai*' is uttered accompanied by ostensive gestures in the direction of rabbits – and then, of course, as Quine makes clear, whether '*gavagai*' is one word is uncertain, just as it is uncertain what word it is. Nor can the interpreter make use of intentions accompanying the speech of those she is attempting to interpret, since guessing their intentions is part of arriving at an interpretation of what is being said. The only way she can proceed is by the familiar inductive first steps of Quinian radical translation.

What Davidson adds to Quine's account of this process is the idea that the hypotheses ventured by the field linguist take the form of T-sentences, or rather, modified T-sentences which relativize truth to times and speakers.[3] The resulting formulations are attempts to capture a three-place predicate intended 'to relate language with occasions of truth in a way that invites the construction of a theory' (*Inquiries*, p. 44). These formulations will look much like this:

(T) '*Gavagai*' is true-in-L when uttered by x at time t if and only if there is a rabbit in the vicinity of x at t.

The interpreter might decide to add 'and the rabbit is being ostensively indicated by x', she might decide the number of rabbits is irrelevant and modify the formulation accordingly, she might even notice that '*gavagai*' is uttered only in fair weather, that a speaker of L cannot be prompted to say '*gavagai*' when it is raining, no matter how many rabbits are splashing conspicuously about, and include this fact as a conjunct in the sentence that is the right side of (T).

Note that she is not trying to *translate* '*gavagai*'. The right side of her conditional is not a guess at what '*gavagai*' *means*. She is trying to formulate a sentence that states as specifically as possible the combination of features characterizing occasions when speakers of L utter '*gavagai*'. On the sole basis of 'facts about the behavior of speakers in relation to sentences' (*Inquiries*, p. 133), in this case '*gavagai*', she must specify the truth-conditions of those sentences as best she can. The hope is to get a sentence or conjunction of sentences that uniquely characterizes these occasions. Collecting a good number of such hypotheses, the interpreter cannot help but discern patterns; she will individuate words, assign them structural roles, and so on.[4] This will allow her to form testable hypotheses, theorems of her nascent theory, that she can try out on the L-speakers: Will they utter the required ss under the circumstances of p?

The process of radical interpretation is intended as a theoretical description of linguistic competence, a rationalization of the practice of interpreting speech, not as a description of an actual procedure such as the methods of translators. And it is easily misconstrued. John Wallace provides an educational example of how *not* to think of radical interpretation in his paper 'Translation Theories and the Decipherment of Linear B' (Wallace, 1986). Wallace believes that careful attention to the way in which Michael Ventris came to decipher the script Linear B as Greek will bring out the inadequacy of the Quine − Davidson model of interpretation. In his reply to Wallace, 'Testing Theories of Interpretations' (Vermazen, 1986), Bruce Vermazen exposes several fundamental problems with the argument. At this point, one in particular should be noted. Wallace complains that contrary to what Quine and Davidson suggest, the 'form in which the meanings of sentences are given is not a simple correlation of sentences to sentences, but this plus a gloss' (Vermazen, 1986, p. 230). However, as Vermazen rightly points out, 'Davidson's truth-theory is required to yield for each foreign sentence a statement of the conditions under which that sentence is true: far from being a mere correlation of a foreign expression with a home expression, such a statement may be just the kind of gloss that Wallace is after ...' (Vermazen, 1986, p. 242). Wallace's mistake is important to expose, because it is so easily made. What underlies it is a misconception of the sense in which a natural language is a given — that it consists somehow of ready-made sentences, of fixed extensions for sentences to have. This is false, and obviously so once it is explicitly stated. What is true is that for any given sentence its extension is fixed. But this is another matter. It places no restrictions on what can be said in a given language, because we are, of course, able to construct new sentences with new extensions. What the radical interpreter is doing is precisely constructing new sentences in her own language to match the extensions given by the sentences of the speakers she is interpreting.

This appears straightforward, but it is not. We quickly slip into reification, thinking of meanings as something to be captured by, but given independently of, the sentences we use. Vermazen himself shows how easily this happens, as he describes Quine's concept of radical translation:

> The linguist will begin by collecting a stock of uninterpreted utterances of his subject, somehow devising a way to turn these utterances into queries (of his own), and then noting his subject's positive and negative responses to queries under various environing conditions. In this way he will build up a catalogue correlating some of the subject's sentences with sensory stimulations caused by things going on around him: a pairing, to use Quine's terminology, of occasion sentences with stimulus meanings. *Translation begins when and if the linguist finds sentences in his own language with the same (or very nearly the same) stimulus meanings.* (Vermazen, 1986, p. 235) [my italic]

What is interesting about Vermazen's description is that it implies that we give the truth-conditions of a sentence and the meaning of a sentence in two separate operations, which is exactly the mistake that Wallace makes. Vermazen implies that our linguist can first describe the 'environing conditions' that produce her subject's assent to a particular sentence, and then go on to see if she has a sentence in her own language that matches those conditions. He even implies that she might conclude that there is no such sentence, that the sentence to which her subject assents cannot be translated into her own language. But then, how would she describe the environing conditions? In describing these conditions, she is *ipso facto* producing the truth-conditions of the sentence, and that is all she has to do to get her theory started. In fact, this is the best way to articulate the task of the radical interpreter: she attempts to isolate the salient features of what Wallace calls the contextual frame in which the uninterpreted sentence is embedded – that is, she attempts to isolate those environing features that cause the speaker to assent to the sentence.

How is this possible? Clearly, our linguist is not forming her tentative T-sentences on the basis of presuppositionless observation. The pure observer would of course never be able to come up with any characterization of occasions of utterance at all. There are at least two assumptions we have to make to get any T-sentence off the ground: First, we have to assume that we are observing creatures who assert, and, crucially, that we are reasonably adept at telling when those observed are engaging in this particular linguistic activity – even when we have no clue as to what is being asserted.[5] Second, we must assume that when they assert, they largely do so correctly. Unless we make both these assumptions, we will never be able to understand what is being said. Let us look at these assumptions one at a time.

That we need to make the first assumption is clear. If we cannot even identify the utterances of L over which the truth-predicate of L ranges, there is no hope of our capturing its extension in T-sentences. And in this case, there would be no chance of bringing out the semantic structure of L *via* a Tarskian theory. But does this mean we need to know the intentions and beliefs of speakers of L before we can construct our theory? If so, we are trapped in a circle. How, Davidson asks, can we know they even *have* beliefs and intentions until we can interpret the sounds they make?

Let us return to our field linguist. In order to pose the question to which (T) is a tentative answer, she has to believe that on her sample occasions, the speakers both intend to utter something true and believe what they utter to be true when they utter it. But she does not know the content of belief, *what* it is the speaker intends to assert, or, precisely, means to say. It is necessary to assume the attitude of holding a sentence to be true on the part of the speaker, but this assumption tells us nothing of intentions and beliefs of a kind useful in determining meaning. And so there is no circle here, we are not sneaking 'meaning' in through our assumptions about beliefs and intentions. We are granting, however, that the subject of our interpretation is a creature with beliefs and intentions. And this means that the causal links the linguist attempts to isolate with her T-sentences run between states of the environing world and intentional states of the subject. What saves the empirical content of the theory is that she can inductively determine these causal links without knowing in advance the particular intentional states of the subject of interpretation.[6]

The significance of the second assumption is not quite so obvious, and it may appear rather implausible. If by insisting on the assumption that their assertions are correct we mean to suggest that the people whose language we are interpreting happen to possess the truth about the world, we would be engaging in a strange form of epistemological occultism. If, on the other hand, we mean to suggest that unless they see the world as we do, unless they believe what we believe, we cannot understand them, we would be not just condoning but insisting on a completely unreflective cognitive parochialism. This last interpretation becomes particularly unpalatable when coupled with the further claim that if we cannot translate a language into our own, there is no language to be translated.

Fortunately, neither of the above construals catch the import of the assumption. It is often called the 'principle of charity', but this is a misnomer in so far as it suggests that it is a principle we magnanimously choose to employ as a kindness toward the native speakers. It is, on the contrary, an indispensable methodological principle, without which, Davidson argues, a theoretical description of our *own* linguistic competence would founder because of the inseparability of attributing beliefs to speakers and meaning to the sentences spoken.

Whatever '*gavagai*' means, whatever the speaker intends to assert, the occasion of assertion can only count as evidence for (T) on the assumption that '*gavagai*' is true to appropriately used. Once we admit the possibility that the speaker of L might falsely assert '*gavagai*' (whatever it means), the conjunct on the right side of (T) is no longer supported by the utterance, because we would be giving up the idea that the observable features of this particular occasion of assertion of '*gavagai*' have any relation to the truth-conditions of '*gavagai*'. Even granting the first assumption, then, that a native speaker's attitude of holding a sentence to be true can be detected by the discerning linguist, this attitude can only serve the linguist's forming of hypotheses like (T) if the native speaker's attitude towards the sentence on a particular occasion is the correct one.

What if the speaker, however, is only pretending to hold a sentence true, or actually does so but is mistaken in her belief? Surely we do not want to rule out mistakes or lies? No, but the point is that the only possible incentive the field linguist could have for attributing error or deceit is that a speaker's utterance of '*gavagai*' conflicts with her inductively acquired T-sentences. And these she could only have formulated by treating as true the native speakers' previous utterances of '*gavagai*' or other expressions in which any structural elements of '*gavagai*' occurred. Certainly the field linguist will be exposed to error and deception, and against a body of strongly supported T-sentences she would probably recognize most of them. But should she be tempted to regard utterances of the subjects of interpretation as systematically false or random, she would merely be depriving her own theory of empirical bite. It is impossible to treat native speakers as anything but on the whole speakers of truth.

Precise articulation of the principle of charity turns out to be an extremely tricky task: Davidson attempts to do so in terms of agreement, but acknowledges that this strategy has not yet succeeded:[7] 'My point has always been that understanding can be secured only by interpreting in a way that makes for the right sort of agreement. The "right sort", however, is no easier to specify than to say what constitutes a good reason for holding a particular belief' (*Inquiries*, p. xvii). The principle of charity serves in one form or another as the foundation for Davidson's much cited arguments against incommensurability and the possibility of our being fundamentally mistaken about how things are.[8] When the premise of these arguments is formulated in terms of a rough and unspecified notion of agreement, it is easy to understand how critics come to regard it as a potential ploy for restricting the label of rationality to those who agree with us. The misunderstanding here surfaces in the implied supposition that the corollary of the principle is that those who do not agree with us are irrational. This, as we will see, does not follow, but as long as exact formulation eludes us, this sort of misconstrual threatens.

Speaking of the principle of charity in terms of agreement and matching beliefs is to think of it only as giving a criterion for evaluating rival theories of interpretation of a language, not as a principle of theory construction. Why? Because until we have such theories, it makes no sense to speak of the interpreter as trying to match her beliefs with those of the speakers of the language she is trying to understand. A belief, Davidson insists, 'is identified by its location in a pattern of beliefs; it is this pattern that determines the subject matter of the belief, what the belief is about' (*Inquiries*, p. 168), just as the meaning of a sentence is given by its location in the structural pattern of the sentences of the language, specified by a theory of truth for the language. Unless we can attribute clusters of beliefs, we cannot attribute beliefs at all. The idea of attributing beliefs one by one is as hopeless as the idea of assigning meaning to sentences in isolation. Hence, no notion of matching beliefs or of agreement will capture the task of interpretation in its initial stages, since at this point there is nothing to which the interpreter can match her beliefs.

The point can be put differently: The concept of belief (and therefore also the concept of agreement) is an intentional concept. And the intentional lies at the other end of our task; the job is precisely to show how we get the intentional from the extensional. Belief and meaning arise in the same way, by the imposition of structure on an infinite supply of extensional evidence. Yet as a methodological principle, the principle of charity must apply also in the initial stages of theory construction. We could say that the interpreter should initially do whatever makes for most agreement in the end, when it does make sense to talk of agreement. But if we take the extensional and holistic nature of our theorizing seriously, we are committed to articulating the assumptions that guide us without intentional concepts like 'belief', 'agreement', and so on. We should also find a way of clearly articulating the problem the principle is intended to solve, the inseparability of belief and meaning, in non-intentional terms. The problem faced by the interpreter is that of establishing a connection between the sentences of L and the observable circumstances of their being uttered. The extensional link is, of course, truth. The first assumption the interpreter needs to make, that she can identify assertions, is now clearly seen not to rest on an attribution of beliefs or intentions to speakers of L. Rather, these attributions are made possible only once the assumption is made that sentences to which truth-value can be ascribed can be identified. But this alone is insufficient. Since the negative truth-value of a sentence severs the connection between sentence and observable circumstance, the interpreter of a language must be able to identify sentences of L with (appropriately relativized) positive truth-value under specific circumstances, in order to link those sentences with the observable features of those circumstances. The principle of charity is intended to express the necessity of presuming that this link obtains for a given sentence.

This assumption appears plain enough, and it is tempting to leave its specification as it stands. But the link between sentences and features of circumstances is the core of Davidson's theory of interpretation, because it is the very transaction in which truth is exchanged for empirical content. And the constituents of this transaction can be analysed further. For this purpose, it will be instructive to ask what it is that goes wrong when the principle of charity is misunderstood.

When misunderstanding occurs, it is mostly due to the failure to hold semantic and anthropological considerations sufficiently separate. To illustrate the importance of the point, let me return to Wallace's attempt to exploit the decipherment of Linear B for philosophical purposes. He acknowledges that theories of radical interpretation are 'intended as analytical or idealized models which have bearing on all communication' (Wallace, 1986, p. 231), and so realizes the tenuous connection between actual instances of interpretation and the validity of the theories. Nevertheless, the Linear B case is one where 'the questions, "What is the evidence?", "How is the evidence marshalled?", "What is the upshot?" have real application' (Wallace, 1986, p. 231). But the answers to these questions are entirely different from what the model of radical interpretation would lead us to expect. Therefore, Wallace believes, it shows the notion of radical interpretation to be without content. In the deciphering of Linear B, he argues, '[t]he distance between evidence and interpretation is stretched almost to the breaking point. Yet we are told that this distance is nothing compared to that which is always being bridged implicitly. But do we understand this at all?' (Wallace, 1986, p. 231).

Actually, the distance we must bridge in deciphering clay tablets is infinitely greater than that faced by the radical interpreter, because the context of utterance is lacking. Without that context, there is no hope of isolating the empirical features of the world which are the causes of the content of the beliefs of the producers of sentences. We could not begin to formulate T-sentences; we would, in principle, not even have any reason to think there was a semantic task to be performed at all. Any interpretation of the tablets is as good as any other; we could regard them as freaks of nature or miracles of God, or as listing prime numbers. Wallace makes this point, but fails to see that what it demonstrates is not the vacuousness of radical interpretation, but the crucial flaw in his own argument. In cracking Linear B, Ventris relied on just the kind of information Quine first designed the situation of radical translation to *exclude*. Ventris had no choice, because he lacked precisely the information which it is the purpose of theories of radical interpretation to isolate. What the Linear B case demon- strates is that interpretation can proceed by way of the theoretical short cuts which are by definition excluded from the repertoire of the radical interpreter. These short cuts are beliefs (psychological, biological, historical, etc.) and conventions that we implicitly rely on to isolate the salient features of contexts of utterance. In the decipherment of Linear B, some such set of beliefs had to be made explicit, serving as it did as the sole basis of interpretation. And this, as Wallace claims, does distinguish it from most normal speech situations, but in this it is not more like radical interpret- ation than ordinary speech, it is *less* so.

If the principle of charity is to serve radical interpretation, we must be extremely cautious lest we use it as a cover for theoretical short cuts. Since it is true that little communication would actually take place without all kinds of social, psychological and linguistic conventions and presuppositions firmly in place, a methodological principle for actual interpretation would inevitably smuggle in assumptions that would obscure the semantic content of the theory of linguistic understanding. Since we are after a theoretical concept of linguistic meaning, we must try to prune our methodological principles of such labour-saving heuristic aids.

For semantics, the confusion between radical interpretation and principles of actual interpretation is fatal. Yet it is not uncommon. Ian Hacking, for instance, in his discussion of Davidson in *Why Does Language Matter to Philosophy* (Hacking, 1975), seems to regard the principle of charity as the common-sense practice of linguists in the field. He says of it and the related principle of humanity: 'There is of course nothing wrong with ... [these principles] ... if they are just commonsense rules of thumb that might, like all common sense, sometimes offer bad advice' (Hacking, 1975, pp. 149–50). This is a two-fold misconstrual. What Hacking is actually describing are the theoretical short cuts available to us as interpreters. They are rules of thumb, in so far as they are made explicit, and they certainly can lead us astray. The principle of charity, on the other hand, offers no *advice* to us as interpreters, it yields no interpretational strategy. It is not a heuristic device, nor is it, accordingly, something we could get by without; it is a *condition of the possibility* of interpretation.

Steven Lukes, in 'Relativism in its Place' (Lukes, 1982) is guilty of the same kind of mistake. He argues that the principle of charity should be replaced with Richard Grandy's principle of humanity:

> The Principle of Charity counseled 'Count them right in most matters'. The Principle of Humanity counsels 'Count them intelligible or perhaps count them right unless we can't explain their being right or can better explain their being wrong'. In other words, it prescribes the minimizing of unintelligibility – that is, of unintelligible agreement and disagreement. It has the singular virtue of being the principle we do in practice apply on the interpretation and translation of beliefs. (Lukes, 1982, p. 262)

Lukes presents the principle of humanity as a 'pragmatic constraint' on interpretation. 'The trouble with unqualified charity is that it bases the necessary agreement on too many truths. Some truths we hold may be ones they could not intelligibly have acquired' (Lukes, 1982, p. 262). He implicitly construes the principle as one to be applied in choosing between alternative existing translation schemes, because it supposedly works on the attribution of beliefs, something which is not possible until some kind of a theory of meaning is in place. And he cheerfully accepts the challenge of spelling out what Davidson refers to as the right kind of agreement in terms of what sorts of beliefs it is reasonable for speakers of a given language to have.

In so far as Davidson lends support to revision of this kind, he obfuscates the significance of the principle, and contributes to a very un-Davidsonian reification of meaning and belief.[9] To understand why, we must make a slight detour.

In chapter 5 we saw that interpretation from one language into another works only because the interpreter possesses a pretheoretical understanding of truth. That is, it works because the interpreter knows how to apply the truth-predicate of her own language. In chapter 2 the point was mentioned that Davidson's strategy for interpretation presupposes that our epistemic judgements are on the whole sound. These points are related to each other, and they are related to the principle of charity; they are both conditions of the possibility of T-sentences having empirical content.

The first point amounts to the requirement that the interpreter understands the language into which another language is to be interpreted. That is, she must know what it is for a sentence of *her* language, the language of the theory (call it TL), to be true. This knowledge is what would be explicitly expressed in a theory of truth for TL. But she has the required pre-theoretical understanding if she knows that some true T-sentences (of the kind that would be generated by a theory of truth for her own language) are appropriate while others, also true, are not, even if she is unable to state the theory that yields only the former as theorems.[10] For example, as a speaker of English she has this understanding if she knows that '"snow is white" is true if and only if snow is white' is appropriate in a way that '"snow is white" is true if and only if grass is green' is not − even though both sentences are true. What she knows is that for a speaker of English the belief expressed by the sentence 'snow is white' is caused by the fact that snow is white, not by the fact that grass is green.

It must be stressed that this understanding is semantic, not epistemic. It is this understanding that allows the interpreter to formulate the right side of the biconditional theorems, the *p* of the T-sentences. But it is not sufficient to know what it is for *p*, a sentence of TL, to be true. She must also know *that* it is true, that it indeed *is true* on the occasions of utterance of the sentence of (L) whose extension she is attempting to capture. That is to say, she must know that it is true on occasions of utterance of *s*. But this epistemic judgement derives no support from the causal relation between her belief and the world. As Davidson says, 'of course we can't get outside our skins to find out what is causing the internal happenings of which we are aware' (Davidson, 1986b, p. 312). This means that the appropriateness of *p* rests on a combination of semantic understanding of the causes of beliefs and epistemic judgement of their coherence.

We saw in chapter 5 how Tarski uses the notion of sameness of meaning to reach a definition of truth for a language. He holds truth for TL and truth for L apart with this lever, and in doing so is able to define truth for L. It was suggested that this notion of truth-for-a-language, though it ensures non-circularity and makes definition possible, somehow resists our intuitive grasp. '*La neige est blanche*' and 'snow is white' are both true, we want to say, without admitting two different truth-predicates. This resistance was acknowledged, but not explained. Now its significance becomes apparent: It is this very intuition of truths-for-languages as somehow *the same* that drives interpretation. Davidson's strategy works by holding truth constant between the languages; T-sentences serve to calibrate TL and L precisely because while the Tarskian characterization of truth is always the characterization of the truth-predicate for a given language, thus bringing out its semantic structure, *truth* is *not* relativized to a language. The concept of truth that underlies a theory of interpretation is a concept of absolute truth.[11] That is to say, in a true T-sentence, *s* and *p* are appropriate to the occasions of empirical observation in the same manner. It is by assuming this sameness of truth, which is the intuitive foundation of Davidson's model of interpretation, that the interpreter is able to understand L. It is by virtue of this trans-liguistic notion that she is able to formulate an empirical theory that in specifying how the truth-conditions of sentences of L are determined by their parts — that is, in characterizing the truth-predicate of the language — actually interprets the language.

The empirical content and explanatory power of a Tarskian theory hinges on the appropriateness of s and p in its theorems. In the case of p, this appropriateness is spelled out in terms of semantic understanding and epistemic judgement. But what of the case of s? The answer is, in exactly the same way. This is, indeed, the point; this is what links s to the circumstances isolated by p. And this *is* the principle of charity.

In interpretation, the semantic understanding embedded in p is linked by the epistemic judgement, that-p to s, through a concept of absolute truth. The assumptions we must make about p and s for this link to be made are the same: that their truth conditions are a product of the structural function of their parts, and that both are true on the occasions that provide empirical evidence for the T-sentence. What a speaker of TL charitably assumes about speakers of L, as a precondition for interpreting what they say, is only what speakers of L would postulate as conditions for regarding someone as a speaker of L in the first place. The principle of charity is just the reverse of what we require of the interpreter herself with respect to TL.

Understanding this relation is seeing that any attempt to spell out the principle of charity is sociological, psychological or anthropological terms is changing the subject. The Quinian model of radical translation, originally designed to isolate the relevant empirical features, is no doubt conducive to this sort of switch in so far as it allows us to forget that what we are discussing is a rationalization not only of the endeavours of the field linguist on an obscure island but also of our homey chatter with the neighbours. But it is nevertheless a different topic. The principle of charity is not a pragmatic constraint on choice between different interpretations, but *a precondition for interpretation*. As a precondition, it also does away with the need for pragmatic constraints like the principle of humanity, for the following reason. The principle of humanity is needed, it is thought, to prevent the attribution of inexplicably held beliefs, particularly beliefs the interpreter takes to be true but regards as somehow inaccessible to the subject of interpretation. As Davidson and Lukes both acknowledge, in formulating such a principle we have to tackle the question of what counts as a good reason for holding a belief. But the question is, how would we come to attribute such odd beliefs in the first place?

By treating sentences of L as true as she is exposed to them, the field linguist provides herself with material for a theory about the structural significance of the elements of sentences of L. As the theory is formed, and she assigns meanings to words, she attributes beliefs in clusters, increasingly sharply defined as her evidential base widens. If she is to individuate a belief of a speaker of L, she must already have a very good idea of the structural role of the terms occurring in the sentence expressing that belief. This she could get only from other sentences in which those terms occur. When she suddenly finds herself crediting the L-speaker with an inexplicable belief, she must have a specific semantic location in the structure of L for the sentence, in so far as she believes she knows what it means, but no similar place for the odd belief in the pattern of beliefs. But how could this happen?

The oddness of the belief presupposes that the interpreter has assigned meaning to the words of the sentence. Hence, she is able to formulate innumerable hypotheses − T-sentences − making use of those words to test her understanding. And in those hypotheses she could presumably express those beliefs, the absence of which makes the inexplicable belief peculiar. In so far as these hypotheses are confirmed, the oddness of the belief would diminish. In so far as they are falsified, the interpreter would have good reason to doubt that her theory assigned the proper structural roles to the terms of the sentence expressing the odd belief.

This might look like a facile answer to a serious worry, but that impression would be misleading. For the answer trades on the crucial point that the radical-interpretation model must be understood as a model of a *process*, not as a model of a static state of semantic competence. More precisely, we might say that semantic competence as it is modelled by radical interpretation is a process, and so cannot be modelled by any one theory of truth. Talking as if any particular, more or less complete, theory of truth might represent a level of semantic competence might lead us to seriously misconstrue the nature of this competence, by ignoring the essentially dynamic nature of semantic understanding.

These considerations also bear on a worry raised in chapter 5, in the discussion of Evans and McDowell. Their problem was this: given a theory of truth T for L, it is always possible to construct a theory T′ which is extensionally indistinguishable from T, yet differs from T in the sense its axioms attribute to the sentences of L. An easy way of constructing what Evans and McDowell called a counterfeit theory is to take a predicate clause of L as designated in T and tack on any contingently true proposition — for instance, as Foster suggests, 'the earth moves' (Foster, 1976, p. 13). So whenever T has L-speakers using the predicate '... is part of ... ' (Foster's example), T′ construes them as also implying 'the earth moves'.

It might appear that to distinguish T from T′, as we certainly must, it is necessary to invoke criteria about the sorts of thing L-speakers can reasonably be interpreted as saying, criteria that are not truth-theoretically defined. But it appears that way only so long as neither T nor T′ already have L-speakers talking about the state of the earth. If we already have L-speakers talking about planetary motion, then we would have structural roles assigned to those words of L that we translate as 'earth' and 'moves' and so on. This would make it possible to deny, in L as interpreted by T, that the predicate ' ... is part of ... ' also implies that the earth moves. We might try to get around this, and produce a counterfeit theory by picking some contingent truth *we* happen to possess but concerning which the L-speakers are as of yet silent. This manoeuver, however, could only work if L was not only a dead language, but a petrified one, in which no new utterances would ever be made. If L, on the other hand, is a natural language, it is in principle never impossible to bring whatever sentence we pick into the evidential base of interpretation, since the scope of a natural language is unlimited. Once we have L-speakers pronouncing upon our chosen contingency, then a comparison of extensional fit will eventually suffice to distinguish the artificial — and false — theory from the real thing, because our theory will have to cope with L-speakers' rejection of our carefully constructed misinterpretation.

Far from being an argument *against* a truth-theoretic conception of meaning, Foster's logical exercise is a good illustration of how linguistic understanding, as modelled by radical interpretation, actually proceeds. In the beginning, any utterance of L could mean anything. Step by step, the interpreter narrows down the options for certain expressions, as she begins to form a theory. How does she do this? Precisely by attempting to eliminate alternative theories on the basis of new evidence. She proceeds, in other words, not so much by a step-by-step construction of one theory as by an ongoing process of exchanging one truth-theory for another, as she gradually widens the scope and refines the grid of meaning.

There is no harm in thinking of radical interpretation as the construction of a theory of truth for a language, as long as we remember that 'the construction of a theory of truth for a language' refers to the endless replacing of one truth-theory with another. If we do not bear this in mind, we will be fooled by the demonstrable inadequacy of any given truth-theory into thinking that we need to introduce additional criteria of theory choice. And the fact is that any one formal truth-theory will always run into trouble. Not only because someone like Foster might come along and come up with clever examples, but simply because any theory will imply all sorts of funny T-sentences as a matter of logic alone. But this is a problem only if we lose sight of the nature of radical interpretation as a process of theory exchange. So long as we regard our grand theory of truth for L as an idealization, and our construction of it as forever a work in progress, we will continue to improve our understanding of L by construing as true as many of their assertions as possible. Attempting to maximize truth, we will continue to replace one inadequate truth-theory with another. That no one theory is ever free of undesired implications is not a problem for the radical-interpretation model. It is what keeps the radical-interpretation process going.

There is, then, no need for a *further* regulating principle beyond the principle of charity, no need to assume anything about speakers of L other than that they *are* speakers of L and generally speak the truth. This is not surprising, when we bear in mind the holistic nature of the attribution of both belief and meaning and the endlessness of the process of interpretation. Odd attributions of belief of the kind Lukes and Grandy are concerned to avoid would signal a weakness in the theory itself; they do not require further constraints on the theory. Strange interpretations of the kind that have Evans, McDowell, Foster and Loar looking for further theoretical constraints merely show up the danger of thinking of natural languages as finite in scope and theories of truth for such languages as even in theory completable.

NOTES

1 This is, as Davidson makes very clear, a close cousin of Quine's radical translation, but differs from the latter in making explicit the assumption that the subject language of the projected translation manual is a language understood by the manual's author. In insisting on interpretation (as meaningful construal of a language) rather than translation (as the mapping of a structural relation, such as we may glean even when we know neither of the languages so related), Davidson retains his focus on semantics, specifically on the relation between structure and meaning. (See *Inquiries*, pp. 126 n., 129–30.)

Radical translation is defined in Quine's *Word and Object* (Quine, 1960, p. 28), and he sets it up similarly in the opening pages of 'Speaking of Objects' (Quine, 1969c), and 'Ontological Relativity' (Quine, 1969a). Davidson makes explicit the fact that it is merely a heuristic device for explicating the nature of all understanding of language: 'The problem of interpretation is domestic as well as foreign: It surfaces for speakers of the same language in the form of the question, how can it be determined that the language is the same? All understanding of the speech of another involves radical interpretation' (*Inquiries*, p. 126). Postulating an ignorant but clever field linguist as interpreter is just intended, as he says, to 'help assumptions from going unnoticed' (*Inquiries*, p. 126), assumptions which are being relied on at this very moment.

2 Proceeding one step at a time, I will stipulate that our interpreter is correctly assuming that she is dealing with one homogeneous language community.

3 Davidson runs through this modification repeatedly (see *Inquiries*, for instance, pp. 34, 43–4, 58, 135–6, 151). The relativization has nothing to do with what we normally think of as a relativist concept of truth, that is, with truth relativized to some scheme or other. On this point see *Inquiries* (p. 68).

4 She will discern *some* pattern, but in cases where the language users are concerned mostly with what to the interpreter are peculiar topics of conversation, she might have to search hard to find a pattern that would get her very far. I will expand upon this point in chapter 9.

5 Davidson has no argument showing that we can make this assumption, apart from the argument that we must make it. Refusing his

please (see *Inquiries*, p. 144), we would either have to deny that interpretation is possible or come up with a different account of it.

6 For some, this is already granting too much. It means that there is no hope of producing a behaviouristic empirical semantics (see Davidson, 1986b, particularly pp. 317—18). But for Davidson, unlike Quine, this was never an ambition (see *Inquiries*, pp. 175—6).

7 Davidson provides variations on the theme in many places, see *Inquiries*, (for example pp. 137, 153, 169, 196—7) and also in his *Essays on Actions and Events*, but here within the framework of a general theory of action (see Davidson, 1980a, pp. 221, 290).

8 The first is of course the topic of 'On the very Idea of a Conceptual Scheme', (*Inquiries*, pp. 183—98), and the second is given explicitly in the so-called 'omniscient interpreter-argument' in 'The Method of Truth in Metaphysics', (*Inquiries*, pp. 199—214), and again in 'A Coherence Theory of Truth and Knowledge' (Davidson, 1986b, p. 317). The common core of these arguments is formulated repeatedly, for instance in 'Radical Interpretation': 'If we cannot find a way to interpret the utterances and other behavior of a creature as revealing a set of beliefs largely consistent and true by our own standards, we have no reason to count that creature as rational, as having beliefs, or as saying anything at all' (*Inquiries*, p. 137).

9 Lukes quotes from 'On the Very Idea of a Conceptual Scheme', (*Inquiries*, p. 196) and Davidson's 'Replies to David Lewis and W. V. Quine' (Davidson, 1974), in order to show that Davidson would be sympathetic to the principle of humanity.

10 See Davidson (1986a, p. 438), where Davidson makes clear the distinction between knowing a language and knowing a theoretical description of that particular competence.

11 Ian Hacking remarks: 'Casimir Lewy [Hacking's teacher] assured me from our first meeting that there was no such thing as true-in-L in life beyond logic. There is just truth' (Hacking, 1986, p. 456). But it should now be clear that it is *because* there is just truth that true-in-L does its semantic work.

7
Radical Interpretation (II): Anomalies and Indeterminacies

We cannot make omniscience on the part of the speakers of a language L a precondition of anyone ever interpreting L. Hence, the interpreter must search for the trivial, where error and dissent are least likely to occur. Search, because she cannot assume a shared notion of triviality. Starting with ostension and middle-sized objects, it is not likely that she will have to search too far, but she can only be reasonably sure she has hit on the obvious for speakers of L when all her informants invariably assert a sentence mentioned on the left side of her hypothesis on occasions described by the right side. But she will have to add, 'and not under other circumstances', because not all obvious truths of L are of use to her. She needs context-sensitive obvious truths. So Davidson agrees with Quine that the initial basis for theory formation will be occasion sentences, or rather, observation sentences – sentences 'on which all speakers of the language give the same verdict when given the same concurrent stimulation' (Quine, 1969b, pp. 86–7). But for Davidson these sentences do not have the special epistemic status Quine wants to give them.[1]

If speakers of L happen to relate to the world much like the interpreter does, finding trivialities will not be very hard. Relevant features characterizing all and only occasions of assertions of 'gavagai' will stand out. If, however, the interpreter can only uniquely describe these occasions with long and awkward conjunctions of seemingly unrelated conjuncts – if after looking long and hard at utterances of what appears to be an observation sentence, she realizes that its truth-conditions are comprised by a large number of seemingly unrelated facts — she can assume that speakers of L relate to the world in ways interestingly different from her own. But there is nothing ineffable about this difference. There is no inexpressible difference between the *p* and *s* that the interpreter vainly attempts to compensate for by adding some kind of gloss to *p*. What is odd about *s* is just that its extension is matched by a sentence that does not come naturally to the interpreter. What is odd about speakers of L, is just that a sentence with this extension appears to come naturally to them.

Should it turn out, for instance, as was suggested above, that L-speakers assert '*gavagai*' only on sunny days, the weirdness of '*gavagai*' would be captured by the T-conditional we get from (T) by adding 'and the weather is nice'. But this oddness will only be captured when the principle of charity is applied to utterances of '*gavagai*'. It might take a lot of evidence to get a field linguist to make this modification, and she might do it reluctantly, only to avoid worse evils like obvious contradictions.[2] But if her theory construction proceeds successfully, she might soon cease to think of '*gavagai*' as an odd way of signalling the presence of a rabbit-in-sunny-weather, and come instead to construe L-speakers as dividing the animal kingdom into two kinds, fair-weather animals and rainy-day animals. Perhaps eventually she, or maybe her children, should she remain in the L-speaking community, might for all practical purposes come to think of the world as populated by such creatures. That would depend on whether they ceased to translate and began to think in L.

Surely, however, we want to object, this is just too bizarre. For a rabbit is a rabbit no matter what the weather is doing. Even to an L-speaker it must be obvious that, if a sudden storm should break out during a rabbit hunt, this does not affect the identity of the rabbits.

There are two points to be made in response. First, it is true that a change in the weather does not affect the identity of what *we* refer to by 'rabbit'. But then, what 'rabbit' refers to is not the same as what '*gavagai*' refers to. That is precisely the point, and that is also the reason why the translation of '*gavagai*' would require a flexible mind. Second, it is no doubt true that there are no language communities that divide the animal kingdom up in this way. But this is only because it is hard to see how they would successfully go about the task of living if they generally relied on criteria of identity of this puzzling sort. We can raise no general theoretical objection to the possibility of different language communities having different ways of picking out objects in the world unless we fall back on some notion of natural kinds, which dictate the reference of our words.

We should remember that the interpreter's incredulous question, 'don't they *see* that it is the same rabbit?' is matched by the L-speakers' equally perplexed outburst (in L, naturally), 'how can she take *that* for a *gavagai*, surely she can tell that it has begun to rain?' Of course she can tell that it is raining, and so she can clearly see that there are no *gavagai* around. But by the same token, if the L-speakers were to speak English, they would unhesitatingly agree that the rabbit remained one and the same – wet, but the same. The difference between the interpreter and the L-speakers is not a difference in what they see and feel, but in what they look for, and in what they deem relevant to something's being a particular something. This will depend on what sorts of features of the world they find it useful to call attention to, juxtapose, or ignore. As it turns out, where the L-speakers live there is a high concentration of a certain strange chemical in the precipitation that temporarily affects hormone production in some animals. Since this in turn has a deleterious effect on the their meat, rabbits are not always edible. *Gavagai*, on the other hand, always taste delicious.

The foregoing discussion makes it clear that the principle of charity does not counsel us to assume that speakers of a language to be interpreted see things the way we do; it is not a tool of cognitive imperialism. Nor is it a rule of thumb, suggesting that on the whole we are likely to assert the same truths. The principle of charity must be applied to interpreter and interpreted alike, if we are to establish the link between utterance and observation on which all interpretation rests. But the principle has no implications about substantive relations between different webs of belief about the world. It is a condition of the possibility of our speaking comparatively about beliefs at all.[3]

Still, human beings being what they are, the assumptions we make about a given utterance in constructing a theory of the semantic structure of a language are in many particular cases false.

No doubt, this is one reason why the principle of charity is sometimes taken to be a rule of thumb or a reasonable guide. But to down-play its significance in this way is to miss the key point that unless the assumptions embodied in the principle of charity are true, the sentence in question and the occasion of its utterance cannot serve as part of the evidential base from which an interpretation of the language is developed. It is only when she has successfully made these assumptions a sufficiently large number of times, when she has developed a theory assigning structural roles to abstracted linguistic atoms and got the quantificational grid pretty much in place, that the interpreter will have any occasion to question their validity in individual instances.[4] These occasions arise when the theory she has developed produces anomalous results, when there is a discrepancy between a theoretical prediction (in the form of a derived T-sentence) of the conditions for asserting a sentence of L, and the actual conditions of its assertion by L-speakers. That there is no one way of responding to or accommodating such anomalies is the source of one, but not the only, form of indeterminacy of interpretation.

The assumptions on which a T-sentence is counted as direct evidence for our interpretation do not hold for all T-sentences observation leads us to formulate. But the evidence will never tell us which T-sentence is the source of the trouble. Once an anomaly appears, it can be pushed around in the theory like a sealed-in airbubble. To understand exactly what it is that is left empirically indeterminate, let us examine in more detail the various options open to an interpreter in the face of anomalies.

The contradiction between evidential base and hypothesis is a matter of conflicting T-sentences: On the basis of our inductively constructed theory of the structure of L, a theorem (T) 's is true if and only if p' falls out deductively, whereas observation gives truth-conditions of the same s that are incompatible with p, say (T1) 's is true if and only if q' (where p and q are contraries). Schematically, there are three possible explanations (on the assumption that we are still working with an idealized homogeneous language community): first, the theory might be deficient; second, the epistemic judgement of L-speakers might be mistaken; third, the epistemic judgement of the interpreter might be mistaken.

To blame the anomaly on the theory, is to declare (T) false. This is what is counselled by the principle of charity, in so far as it is simply the application to theories of interpretation of the general principle of all theory construction that empirical content be maximized. It is to say that the meaning of s was not understood, because the structural significance of its parts were misconstrued by the theory. We might be able to debug our theory by changing, for instance, the reference of one of the words in s, and so both resolve the anomaly and increase our evidential base. The result will be not just a new understanding of s, but an adjustment in our understanding of L as a whole. The effects of such tampering ripple through the theory, though they diminish towards the infinitesimal with the increasing remoteness of sentences from s in the semantic structure of L. But unless there is a perfect epistemological match between interpreter and interpreted, we will reach a point where this kind of tinkering with the theory to deal with one maverick inductive T-sentence will result only in the escape from the herd of another. Once we get beyond the initial, tentative steps of theory formation, it will quickly become impossible to incorporate in a consistent theory all the inductive evidence that we at any given point possess. So we are forced to exclude some of it.

How do we exclude apparent evidence? By attributing error. The diligent interpreter will first of all recheck (T1), just in case q should turn out to be false. If she cannot dismiss q, she has no choice but to discount the evidential relevance of (T1) by suspending the principle of charity in this particular case. By declaring s false, she can retain both (T) and q as true, thus saving both her theory — that is, her understanding of L — and her world view — that is, her belief that q. But the price is the loss of part of the evidential base, one small empirical suction cup.[5]

In those cases where empirical content is maximized and the price must be paid, we are faced with a choice of how to pay it, which T-sentences to sacrifice. A third-century Roman peasant might come away from a time-travelling astronomer's attempt to demonstrate the shape of the earth wondering what is wrong with this odd individual who thinks that oranges are flat. Once an interpreter gives up accommodating someone's holding a sentence true by altering the location we assign to it in the structural pattern brought out by the theory, she can only do so by attributing a false belief to the speaker. Indeed, on Davidson's view this is the very function of the concept of belief:

> The distinction between a sentence being held true and being in fact true is essential to the existence of an interpersonal system of communication, and when in individual cases there is a difference, it must be counted as error. Since the attitude of holding true is the same whether the sentence is true or not, it corresponds directly to belief. The concept of belief thus stands ready to take up the slack between objective truth and the held true, and we come to understand it in just this connection. (*Inquiries*, p. 170)

The attitude of holding-to-be-true is a vector, as Davidson puts it, of two forces, the meaning of the sentence and the belief expressed by it. Knowing one, we should know the other. But of course, the problem is that we know neither. Davidson describes his strategy as that of holding belief constant while solving for meaning. It is important here that we do not reify belief, but see it as the derivative concept it is (at least for semantic purposes). We use it to accommodate discrepancies, not just between interpreter and the idealized interpreted — the homogeneous language community — but also discrepancies between speakers of the same language. In fact, it is only by invoking the concept of belief that we are able to say that they *are* speakers of the same language in spite of the variations between them. We streamline their speech behaviour by attributing the occasional idiosyncratic false belief (or discount the utterance as not being a proper assertion at all), and this allows us to construe what they say by means of the same truth theory.

Once we are forced to let go of truth and open up the play of meaning and belief, we can account for the attitude of a speaker to a sentence in indefinitely many ways. It might be thought that here a use for something like the principle of humanity can be found: in choosing between theories that use the same proportion of the inductively established T-sentences as evidential support, and accounting for the remaining set of sentences anomalously held true by attributing false beliefs, we should pick the one that makes the speakers in some sense most reasonable. But this idea is barren, no matter how we rank the reasonableness of beliefs. It is barren, because the anomalies are expressions of discrepancies between patterns, between structures, not between beliefs held individually. We are not told which T-sentence is the source of the trouble because no one T-sentence *is* the source of the trouble. Two theories sacrificing different parts of the evidential base may simply be alternative ways of stating the discrepancy.

They *may* be, yet the idea that any two such theories of interpretation are empirically equivalent is often hard to swallow. Whether we take *s* to mean 'oranges are flat' and *r* to mean 'the earth is flat', or whether we interpret them as predicating roundness of these objects, is surely a question that makes a difference: 'This strange person is saying either that both the earth and oranges are round, or that they are both flat. In either case there is a weird mistake, but they are different mistakes, or my name is not Gaius.' Yet it is conceivable (barely) that for a flat-earther the two respective theories have what we might call the same empirical wealth.[6] Certainly we would resist saying that there is *no* difference in meaning no matter which theory we use to construe the sentences. But this is what we should say, if we take seriously the idea that a difference of meaning ultimately must be a matter of empirical distinguishability, and there are no further empirical determinants.

It might look as if this is where Davidson leaves us: 'When all the evidence is in, there will remain, as Quine has emphasized, the trade-offs between the beliefs we attribute to a speaker and the interpretations we give his words. But the resulting indeterminacy cannot be so great but that any theory that passes the tests will serve to yield interpretations' (*Inquiries*, p. 139). If there is no choosing between two theories in terms of their empirical wealth, they are both acceptable solutions even if they account for the evidence in different, sometimes incompatible, ways. A sentence held true on one scheme might in the same circumstances be held false on the other, provided adjustments are made elsewhere in the theory. Hacking argues that Davidson is leaving too much scope for indeterminacy here, in a way that involves him in a contradiction:

> [Indeterminacy of this sort implies that] ... there will be nothing to choose between a T-sentence '*s* is true if and only if *p*', provided in one system, and '*s* is true if and only if *q*', provided

in another system. Yet we had the initial overriding requirement that T-sentences are true. Since *p* and *q* may be contraries, *both* T-sentences cannot be true. From Davidson's standpoint, this is a *reductio ad absurdum* of indeterminacy. (Hacking, 1975, p. 154)

Even if this argument went through, it would not make Davidson what Hacking calls a 'just-righter', because certain kinds of indeterminacy remain even when truth is held constant between two theories. In any case, the argument rests on an error, pointed out by Davidson in an explicit response: 'Our mistake was to suppose there is a unique language to which a given utterance belongs' (*Inquiries*, p. 239). Though Davidson brings it up in a by-the-way manner, the point is essential. What is indeterminate is not what a sentence of a language means, *but what language is being spoken*. If this seems like a splitting of semantic hairs, it is because we are not considering the relation between Hacking's mistake and the reification of meaning. The mistake comes easily to all of us, in so far as we remain influenced by the idea that individual sentences must have their own determinate meanings, that there is something that determines what language someone speaks prior to the empirical task of systematizing the semantic structure of someone's speech behaviour. Once the full import of Davidson's holistic empirical strategy has soaked in, we will not make this mistake, because we will see that the only possible criterion of identity for languages is the successful application of one and the same theory of truth. Since we never apply the exact same theory to any two speakers, or even to any one speaker at different points in time, this makes the identity of languages a matter of degree.

Although it is not for the reason Hacking believes he sees, Davidson does not leave much room for indeterminacy between languages of the sort we have discussed. We have some reason for our intuitive difficulty in accepting that there is nothing to choose between theories ascribing incompatible truth-conditions to the sentences held true by speakers of L. What Davidson really has his eye on is a theory not just of speech behaviour, but of behaviour *per se*, a unified theory of meaning and action (cf. Davidson, 1980b). He says: '[I]ndeterminacy [of meaning or translation] is important only for calling attention to how the interpretation of speech must go hand in hand with the interpretation of action generally, and so with the attribution of desires and beliefs' (*Inquiries*, p. 154). Not just the holding-to-be-true of sentences but actions generally can be explained through the attribution of beliefs. The vector of forces here is constituted by belief and desire. A given action can be explained by an indeterminate number of different combinations of the two. A further empirical constraint is imposed on a general theory of action by the demand that it render beliefs attributed on the basis of speech behaviour consistent with the beliefs attributed through decision-theoretic evaluations of action. Davidson believes this will narrow down the choice between alternative theories to the extent that indeterminacy will no longer be a concern. Our intuitive difficulty with indeterminacy of meaning is explained by the fact that our intuition is informed by an interpretation not just of what a person says, but also of what he or she does.[7]

At this point it is worth making a brief digression relating back to the theme of chapter 3, the conflict between reference-based semantics and holism. For an important element in Fodor's resourceful campaign to make meaning holism seem, on the whole, less attractive than building-block semantics, is precisely the claim that the holist has no recourse to the explanation of behaviour in terms of beliefs and desires, whereas such explanations square nicely with causal theories of reference. Semantic holism, according to Fodor, is 'entirely destructive of the hope for a propositional attitude psychology' (Fodor, 1987, p. 56). This is a serious worry. If there can be no 'modus vivendi between Meaning Holism and intentional psychology' (Fodor, 1987, p. 59) – that is, if a commitment to holism blocks the possibility of psychological explanations that rely on the attribution of beliefs and desires – then a lot of people would, understandably, get off the holistic raft.

I am going to back off from most of the intricate questions in the philosophy of mind that now loom alarmingly on the horizon. I will suggest, however, that to substantiate his charge, Fodor is going to need a more elaborate argument than the one he provides. That argument is based on the following two characterizations:

Meaning Holism is the idea that the identity – specifically, the intentional content – of a propositional attitude is determined by the totality of its epistemic liaisons. (Fodor, 1987, p. 56).

When an intentional system takes the semantic value of P to be relevant to the semantic evaluation Q, I shall say that P is an *epistemic liaison* of Q (for that system at that time). (Fodor, 1987, p. 56)

Adding to this the plausible premise that no two organisms ever hold exactly the same set of circumstances to be relevant to the determination of the truth value of a particular proposition, Fodor concludes that 'it's going to turn out de facto that no two people ... ever *are* in the same intentional state' (Fodor, 1987, p. 57). And this spells big trouble for intentional psychologies, which 'achieve generality ... by *quantifying over all the organisms that are in a specified intentional state*' (Fodor, 1987, p. 57).

However, this is just a little too quick. It is not clear that semantic holism commits us to a way of identifying beliefs that preclude the sharing of intentional states. Certainly, for the holist, to ascribe one belief is to ascribe many. This does not, naturally, preclude the identification of a believer's individual beliefs. The question is, does it preclude the possibility of ascribing the *same* belief to two (or more) different believers, like Smith and Jones, or Jones at time T_1 and Jones at time T_2? Contrary to Fodor, I suggest that it does not, even though different believers may typically semantically evaluate a shared belief by different routes.

The reason is this: the bearing of what the *believers themselves take to be relevant* to the semantic evaluation of a belief on the identity of that belief is less direct than Fodor presupposes; it is, crucially, mediated by an *interpreter*. The concept of a belief is one that arises in the *interpretation of* the believer. The *intentional content* of a belief is given by the proposition that expresses it, for example 'Blackie is a horse'. What other propositions various believers take to have bearing on whether Blackie is indeed a horse, is important to the content of this belief in so far as it gives an *interpreter* a way of figuring out what they *mean* when they say 'Blackie is a horse'. Of course, what different believers deem relevant in assessing the truth-value of 'Blackie is a horse' *may* turn out to undermine the idea of a shared belief, but not in the way Fodor thinks. For if Smith and Jones appear to semantically evaluate the proposition 'Blackie is a horse' by way of puzzlingly different sets of epistemic liaisons, this will *not* lead us to conclude that Jones's belief that Blackie is a horse is different from Smith's belief that Blackie is a horse, or that sameness of belief is a matter of degree. It will lead us to conclude that we have got the meaning of the phrase 'Blackie is a horse' wrong in at least one case. Perhaps Jones believes that Blackie is a pony. If so, this does not preclude the possibility of quantifying over organisms with the belief that Blackie is a horse, it only suggests that it would be a mistake to count Jones as one of them.

If on an interpreter's best theories of Smith and Jones they both *mean* that Blackie is a horse when they sincerely assert (or somehow token) 'Blackie is a horse', then they share that particular belief, even if the interpreter's best overall theory about what Jones means and believes will be different from her best overall theory about what Smith means and believes. As long as Smith and Jones both come out believing that Blackie is a horse, they are, for the purposes of cognitive psychology, in the same intentional state, even though they may well have different grounds for being in it, and even though we as intepreters cannot attribute this belief to them except in the context of our (different) theories of what the (different) grounds for their belief are.

So holists are entitled to do what indeed everyone must do when trying to explain what people say and do, namely attribute beliefs and desires and quantify over organisms that share particular ones. But, to return to the main topic of this chapter, do such explanations eliminate indeterminacy altogether? No, they do not, for two reasons. First, the same sort of indeterminacy I talked about before would still appear, since none of us are perfectly consistent and omniscient. There would still be tensions between the need for a consistent theory and the inductively gathered evidence. As David Lewis says in 'Radical Interpretation', it arises 'because no solution fits all the constraints perfectly, and many different ways to strike a balance give many different compromise solutions' (Lewis, 1974, p. 343).[8] The underlying conviction is that the extent to which the language of a speaker is left indeterminate when all their behaviour is taken into account, not just their utterances but their acts as well, would not be intuitively troubling. This is no happy accident, of course. Both Davidson and Lewis take the presence of intuitive resistance to the empirical indeterminacy between concrete theories as an indication that we in practice have more constraints on our interpretation of persons than are captured by the theoretical rationalizations. When there is maximal recognition of all the empirical constraints, the alternative ways of accommodating anomalies should be unworrying. If we do feel that something is lost between empirically equivalent theories, this means either that there are more constraints to be discovered or that the empirical-holistic theory of meaning is false. As Lewis says:

> *Credo*: If ever you prove to me that all the constraint we have yet found could permit two perfect solutions, differing otherwise than in the auxiliary apparatus of M [the truth-theory], then you will have proved to me that we have not yet found all the constraints. (Lewis, 1974, p. 343)

As I stressed in chapter 6, in constructing a truth-theory for a natural language, there is always more evidence to be had. The empirical constraints never run out.

There is another reason why indeterminacy is unavoidable, apart from our proneness to error and erratic behaviour. This is the semantic equivalent of Quine's thesis of the inscrutability of reference, which Davidson discusses in a paper appropriately called 'The Inscrutability of Reference' (*Inquiries*, pp. 227–41; cf. Quine, 1969a). The point can be demonstrated by imagining two consistent and omniscient beings who suffer from the one imperfection that they do not speak one another's language. When they engage in mutual interpretation, no notion of belief will ever crop up, because there is no error or epistemic inconsistency to accommodate, no evidence, that is, that needs to be counted out to preserve the consistency of the theory. Here truth is invariant, the problem of the vector disappears, and the kind of linguistic indeterminacy discussed so far will not arise. When no evidence need be excluded, there can be no choice as to what evidence to exclude. There is no need for compromise, since there is no discrepancy.

Indeterminacy still arises, however, because any set of T-sentences can be produced from different axiomatic bases. These differences can be of two kinds: '[The] logical form may be indeterminate: two satisfactory theories may differ in what they count as singular terms or quantifiers or predicates, or even with respect to the underlying logic itself' (*Inquiries*, p. 228). Though the quantificational grid is brought down in one fell swoop, it can be brought down in different ways to similar effect. The nonlogical axioms may also differ. The references assigned to words by one theory may be altered by permutations to produce another in a manner that does not effect the structural relations between the terms. And as long as these are preserved, the theorems of the theories will be identical (see *Inquiries*, p. 229).

Nothing one omniscient consistent being can say or do will give the other grounds for choosing one permutation over another.[9] Is there something, then, that even omniscient beings do not know? No, because the indeterminacy of omniscience expresses the point that no matter how extensive our theory has become, 'alternative ways of stating the facts remain open' (*Inquiries*, p. 154).[10] Ultimately, which theory these beings should employ is not entirely an empirical question. Since the same pattern of sentences is produced by the same structural relations of their parts on any theory which fits the evidence, nothing of significance is lost in choosing between the languages defined by the theories. This is not so much a consequence of a holistic theory of meaning as its central assumption: When Davidson says that the meaning of a sentence 'is given by assigning the sentence a semantic location in the pattern of sentences that comprise the language' (*Inquiries*, p. 225), he is not claiming to have come up with an ingenious device for getting at the meanings of sentences. He is claiming that this is the only content the notion of meaning has.

NOTES

1 For more on occasion sentences, see Quine (1960, pp. 35–45). For more on the distinction between occasion sentences and the subset Quine dubs observation sentences, see also his 'Empirical Content' (Quine, 1981a); 'Use and its Place in Meaning' (Quine, 1981c); 'Epistemology Naturalized' (Quine, 1969b, particularly pp. 86–7). Davidson does not think we can attribute any particular epistemological status to observation sentences because this presupposes that we can spell out the notion of a speaker's verdict in behaviouristic terms as well as provide a physicalistic description of the 'the same concurrent stimulation' as an intermediary between objects in the world and objects of our beliefs. Davidson does not think we can do either.

2 In 'On the Very Idea of a Third Dogma' (Quine, 1981b), Quine proposes that changes in the length of sentences under translation might serve as the basis for defining a measure of the conceptual distance between languages.

3 Thus Davidson writes:

It isn't that any one false belief necessarily destroys our ability to identify further beliefs, but that the intelligibility of such identifications must depend on a background of largely unmentioned and unquestioned true beliefs. To put this another way: the more things a believer is right about, the sharper his errors are. Too much mistake simply blurs the focus. (*Inquiries*, p. 168)

The reason is clear: the larger the evidential base successfully incorporated in the theory, the more precise will be the structural roles assigned to the words of the language, and the richer meaning will be.

4 The logical grid is brought down, as Davidson says, 'in one fell swoop' (*Inquiries*, p. 136). One might ask: But what if their logic is different from ours? Again, we would only have occasion to wonder about this after we have been largely successful in fitting our logic on to their linguistic behaviour. The reason is the constraints imposed by convention T: if there is no quantificational structure, there is no Tarski-style theory, and hence no theorems to be tested. Certainly, the recursive axioms and the axioms mapping variables to objects (assigning reference to terms) are nothing but theoretical postulates which gain content only from their effect on the truth-value of sentences, but they nevertheless constitute the interpretation. So whatever is required for the recursive characterization of satisfaction, is required for interpretation. This is why Davidson's views on the possibility of indeterminacy of logical structure are more restrictive than Quine's. (See *Inquiries*, p. 228.)

5 Note that the two alternatives are not symmetrical. From the point of view of the theory maker, finding fault with q is more productive than declaring s false, because the latter necessarily counts (T1) out as direct evidence for the theory, whereas the former does not. A source of motivation to challenge one's own beliefs is therefore intrinsic to the interpretational enterprise itself.

6 This problem is different from that raised by Evans and McDowell. In the latter case, the alternative theories were extensionally equivalent, but intuitively irreconcilable. In the present case, the theories are *not* truth-theoretically equivalent, since they make different sentences come

out true, but they are empirically on a par in the sense that the *proportion* of the evidence they consistently account for is the same.

7 The parallel and relation between the belief – desire vector in decision theory and the belief – meaning vector in semantics is discussed in 'Belief and the Basis of Meaning', in *Inquiries* (pp. 141–54).

8 By radical interpretation Lewis means not just the construal of linguistic behaviour, but the interpretation of persons generally, that is, he takes it to refer to what Davidson calls a unified theory of meaning and action.

9 The untestability of the building-block attempts to fix reference (discussed in chapter 3) is the mirror image of this inscrutability.

10 For this very reason, Davidson does not think that the inscrutability of reference calls for a relativizing of ontology, 'since [the latter notion] suggests that, when enough decisions, arbitrary or otherwise, have been made, unique reference is possible, contrary to our argument for the inscrutability of reference' (*Inquiries*, p. 235).

8
What is a Language?

We can regard Davidson's conception of meaning as the result of two theoretical inversions. The first, as we saw in chapter 3, is his turning upside down the building-block approach to linguistic meaning. For Davidson, the source of the signifying power of a word and of the possibility of effecting a speech act with a sentence is located in the totality of the language to which they belong. The second inversion, discussed in chapter five, lies in his suggestion that we use a Tarskian theory of truth to make explicit the manner in which words and sentences draw that power from the pattern of which they are a part. For Davidson makes use of Tarski's work only by making truth, the very concept Tarski intended to illuminate, the foundation of his theory.

In chapter 6 I argued that the empirical content of such a theory suffices for it to yield a theoretical description of what it is we know when we understand the literal meanings of the words of a language. It became clear that a theory of meaning of this kind can never be couched in purely behaviouristic terms, involving as it does the ascription of the irreducibly intentional 'holding true'. However, I argued, contrary to current orthodoxy among semanticists, the theory *can* be framed without the need for constraints on the evidential base other than the maximizing of true theorems. In other words, though it is assumed from the outset that the theory applies to creatures with intentional states, the machinery of the theory is wholly extensional.

A consequence of this, which appeared in chapter 6, is that if we want to know what a speaker means, we have no choice but to treat him/her as on the whole a speaker of truth. I stress again that this is not a *credo* of some kind; it is not an expression of faith in the sincerity or the epistemic acumen of speakers. Just as we have no choice, if we want to make sense of what others say, but to regard them as on the whole speaking the truth, so we have no choice but to regard *ourselves* as largely speakers of truth. The principle of charity is no overestimation of our cognitive and communicative capacities. Massive error, just like massive deception, presupposes an epistemic, representational relation between language and the world and a corresponding reification of the meanings of words and sentences. And this is the very conception of language which Davidson urges us to let go. On the radical-interpretation model of language, the meanings of assertions are not to be construed in terms of *representations* of some non-linguistic reality. They cannot, *a fortiori*, be systematically inadequate representations of reality.

The unfortunately named principle of charity appears charitable only when we forget that the insight an interpreter gleans when isolating the causal relations between the world and a speaker's beliefs is *semantic*, not epistemic, and that these causal relations are not available for justificatory purposes (see Davidson, 1986b, p. 314; 1986c, p. 332). Once we come to see the relation between language and word as a causal semantic relation, the principle of charity just becomes the expression of the naturalistic view of what it is for words to mean that I have been explicating and defending.

What Davidson wants is to illuminate meaning in terms of a theoretical description of linguistic competence. At the end of chapter 7, it appeared as if one were within reach. Is linguistic competence not simply the knowledge of a given language L as rationalized by a Tarskian theory of truth for L?

This conclusion would be mistaken. For what is it we know when we know a language? What is this L? Throughout, I have been proceeding as if the identity of L could always be established, that L was always somehow given: though she does not *know* L, the field linguist at least knows that L is the language to be learned. But once the full import of Davidson's holistic empirical strategy has soaked in, we see that the only possible criterion of identity for languages is the successful application of one and the same theory of truth. For Davidson, there is no way in which a language, as that which a speaker makes use of when successfully communicating, can be given independently of the truth-theory that determines its structure. This is why Davidson conceives of any indeterminacy of translation as an indeterminacy as to what language is being spoken.

Now we must ask, can we simply identify the concept of a language with the L in the formula 'true-in-L' that is the core of a Tarskian theory of truth? The concept of a language as given by true-in-L was, as I suggested in chapter 1, the board on which Davidson stood while developing a theory of meaning without meanings. But this board, too, turns out to be in need of replacement. The concept of a language is itself a reification. For we never apply the exact same theory to any two speakers, nor even to any one speaker at different points in time, since the construction of a theory of truth for a natural language is not a completable process. And this has led Davidson to reject, first, the idea that traditionally conceived convention plays any essential role in linguistic communication (see *Inquiries*, pp. 265–80), and, more recently, also the idea that the concept of a language can be given theoretical content (see Davidson, 1986a).

Neither of these conclusions follows obviously from the premise that no two individuals, nor any one individual at different times, are likely to use words in exactly the same way. I know of no one who would dispute the latter, but few are willing to draw the conclusions from this that Davidson does. Why, then, does Davidson dismiss convention as having no semantic significance?

A convention is an intentional conformity to a regularity. It involves, as David Lewis explains, among other things, the nested beliefs of the conveners in their mutual intent to conform and their belief that this common intent gives each of them good reason to conform.[1] It also presupposes the possibility that the point of the convention could have been achieved by conformity to some regularity other than the one that actually constitutes the convention. The concept of convention would thus appear to be exactly what is needed in explaining why speakers of Spanish use '*la nieve es blanca*' rather than, for example, '*snøen er hvit*' to indicate to their fellows that snow is white, and why it is they thereby have an excellent chance of realizing their communicative intent. So for instance, Appiah, in his polemic against Dummett, uses Lewis's analysis of convention in providing what he takes to be the basics of a realist account of meaning: 'Now that we know what it is for a regularity to be conventional, all that is needed for our purposes is to say what regularity you must conform to in order to know the language of a certain linguistic community' (Appiah, 1986, pp. 10–11). On this approach, each of the theorems in a theory of truth for L would capture a convention conformed to by L-speakers. The mastery of a language, and hence linguistic competence, is therefore the mastery of a set of conventions. Dummett and Appiah agree on this point, though they disagree strongly as to whether it is truth-conditions or assertibility-conditions that are conventionally given.

Davidson thinks this is wrong, for the simple reason that communication *does* succeed without the kind of regularity in the use of language that the conventional account presupposes. In 'A Nice Derangement of Epitaphs', he introduces a distinction between what he calls 'prior' and 'passing' theories, and uses this distinction to show that whatever it is we know that allows us to understand each other's speech, it cannot be knowledge of conventions. The interpreter's prior theory 'expresses how he is prepared in advance to interpret an utterance of the speaker' (Davidson, 1986a, p. 442), while the prior theory of the speaker 'is what he *believes* the interpreter's prior theory to be' (Davidson, 1986a, p. 442). These need not coincide for communication to succeed. In fact, no prior theory is necessary, as the exercise of the field linguist suggests. Speakers' actual usage does not have to conform to our expectations of their usage as a condition for our understanding what is meant. By focusing on malapropisms and idiosyncratic language use, Davidson shows that our everyday conversations require more non-homophonic interpretation than we might think. His claim is, in effect, that even if we used *nothing but* malapropisms, communication would still be possible. As field linguists, we understand each other without having to make any assumptions about whether this or that language is spoken. So even if one were to argue that our prior theories do constitute a body of conventions, this would not show that linguistic communication is essentially conventional. Communication does occur even though no such convention-based theory is ever completely right, and can in principle occur even when such a theory is absent altogether.

What must coincide for an interpreter to understand a speaker are their respective *passing theories*. But, Davidson argues,

> the passing theory cannot in general correspond to an interpreter's linguistic competence. Not only does it have its changing list of proper names and gerrymandered vocabulary, but it includes every successful − i.e. correctly interpreted − use of any word or phrase, no matter how far out of the ordinary. Every deviation from ordinary usage, as long as it is agreed on for the moment (knowingly deviant, or not, on one, or both, sides), is in the passing theory as a feature of what the words mean on that occasion. Such meanings, transient though they be, are literal . . . (Davidson, 1986a, p. 442)

Passing theories are, in other words, just that − passing. There is, then, nothing that constitutes a conventional regularity. This means that the literal meanings of words are not secured by any conventional connection, whether it be construed as a connection between sentences and particular uses of sentences or between words and particular extensions or intensions of words.

One might argue here that what follows from the success of the field linguist, in establishing the literal meaning of what is said without the use of conventions, is not that *no* conventions need be adhered to, only that the field linguist and the subjects of her interpretation need not conform to the *same* conventions. One could then read each successive truth-theory arrived at by the interpreter in the process of communication as a way of spelling out what the set of linguistic conventions of her subjects is on any given occasion. The radical-interpretation model could then be seen as a rationalization of the process whereby we come to *learn* the conventions of a language, rather than a model of what it is we do when we, as masters of a language, make use of that language. It would still, one might claim along these lines, be a matter of convention that a certain noise and not another signifies, say, 'epithet'. So when Mrs Malaprop says 'epitaphs' in referring to what most of us would call epithets, 'epitaphs' has the unusual meaning it has by convention, even if this convention is conformed to only by Mrs Malaprop, and even if she should conform to it only on this occasion. But is this not a *reductio* of the notion of a convention? If we allow a convention to be a convention even when it is conformed to only by a single speaker, a speaker who is constantly changing her conventions, of what use will the concept be in a theory of meaning?

In my view, we are tempted to introduce conventions in semantics in part because conventions appear to be a way of tying together speaker, hearers and words; the concept dovetails nicely with our vague intuition that linguistic communication works when the communicators somehow understand *the same thing* by the tokens they use. It seems to me that much semantic theory has been an attempt to make sense of this intuition. This would explain why conventions are an essential part of seemingly very different semantic approaches, such as Appiah's and Dummett's. On the view I am arguing for, the need for conventions to explain meaning is another aspect of the reification of meaning. It is only if we see meaning as something to be *captured* in the words we use, and conveyed by them from one speaker to another, that we think there must be something connecting the speakers, something – such as a language – they share, that bears meanings as a vehicle.

In any case, conventions could only serve this (regressive) purpose as long as they are *shared*. Once we allow conventions to be neither regularities, since they can change from moment to moment, nor shared, since they might be manifested only in one idiosyncratic idiolect, there is no longer much content to the claim that a theory of linguistic meaning must involve conventions. It is true that we could have used sounds and signs to mean or refer to what we are talking about other than the sounds and signs we actually do happen to use. But to deny that words mean what they do by virtue of the conventions we have adopted, is not to deny this obvious fact. As Davidson says, 'while what is conventional is in some sense arbitrary, what is arbitrary is not necessarily conventional' (*Inquiries*, p. 265). That French speakers use '*la neige*' and German speakers '*der Schnee*' to refer to snow is *semantically arbitrary* in this sense: none of the many interesting facts about language that might explain this and other differences between French and German are facts that tell us anything about how to understand these languages.

However, even if what was captured by a truth-theory for L *were* conventional in nature, the radical-interpretation model does not, contrary to what Davidson originally had thought, rationalize our linguistic competence as knowledge of Tarskian theories of truth for languages. The essential competence turns out to be the ability to continuously form and reform such theories by interpreting assertions as on the whole true. The knowledge rationalized by any one given passing theory — the knowledge of a language, if we like — is fleeting, and, beyond the particular occasion of utterance to which it is applied, utterly without theoretical worth. As communicative exchange proceeds, as language is used in monologue or dialogue, what keeps an interpreter in the game is not any one theory, but the ability to come up with new ones. Linguistic competence on Davidson's view is essentially dynamic and creative and no more subject to theoretical rationalization than theory formation generally. We derive our passing theories, Davidson observes: 'by wit, luck, and wisdom ... There is no more chance of regularizing, or teaching, this process than there is of regularizing or teaching the process of creating new theories to cope with new data in any field — for that is what this process involves' (Davidson, 1986a, p. 446). As he puts it in 'Communication and Convention':

> No doubt we normally count the ability to shift ground appropriately as part of what we call 'knowing the language'. But in this sense, there is no saying what someone must know who knows the language; for intuition, luck, and skill must play as essential a part here as in devising a new theory in any field: and taste and sympathy a larger role. (*Inquiries*, p. 279)

Hence, even if one insisted that the theorems of a truth-theory were true by convention, one still would not have shown that linguistic competence can be described as conventional, since knowledge of the conventions would be neither necessary nor sufficient for communication to succeed. It would not be necessary, since radical interpretation proceeds without such knowledge; it would not be sufficient, since an interpreter equipped only with an immutable truth-theory would understand correctly only a transitory idiolect, and would very quickly get any actual speaker wrong. Even if it were granted that any given truth-theory captures a set of conventions, the continuous production of such theories cannot be described as a matter of conforming to conventions of meaning.

It follows that communication does not depend, as we naturally tend to suppose, on our speaking the same language. Radical interpretation will in principle succeed as long we regard speakers as generally speaking the truth, continuously reforming our theories of meaning on that assumption.

Dummett has taken issue with this dismissal from semantics of the concept of convention and the concomitant rejection of the idea of a language constituted by conventions. A language, Dummett objects, 'is an existing pattern of communicative speech: it is not a theory, but a phenomenon' (Dummett, 1986, p. 467). As Dummett sees it, we all have our own evolving idiolects, and no one idiolect perfectly matches a language. But idiolects can be related in ways which make it plausible to claim that they are idiolects of the *same language*. This language, as an existing pattern, is a social practice, and as such is specifiable in terms of the conventions that constitute it. The fact that no one idiolect embodies all the conventions at all times does not make any difference: these conventions are inductive generalizations over a number of speakers or idiolects, and are no less real because the pure language constituted by them is both an idealization and in constant change.

None of this is actually inconsistent with Davidson's views. He does not deny that there *are* conventions involved in communication, only that there necessarily and in principle must be. In practice, there certainly are regularities of idiolects that dispose us to group them into natural languages. What Davidson doubts is that the concept of a language *in this sense* can throw any theoretical light on linguistic meaning. And here is where he and conventionalists like Lewis, Appiah and Dummett differ. For they take it that linguistic communication does essentially involve conventions. They think that what allows one English speaker to understand another is just the fact that the interpreter interprets the speaker as speaking an idiolect of English. So if the English language were not meaningful independently of all the individual speakers' idiosyncratic versions of it, no understanding would be possible. For Davidson, on the other hand, rule-governed repetition is 'a usual, though contingent, feature' (*Inquiries*, p. 280) of speech. Our theories of meaning apply primarily to occasions of utterance, not to this or that language, nor, for that matter to this or that idiolect.

The latter point warrants some clarification because one might get the impression that the points I have been stressing in the present chapter trade on a distinction between idiolects and languages. But this is not the case. The salient contrast is not that between idiolects and languages, but between *occasions of utterance*, on the one hand, and abstractions, such as languages or idiolects, on the other. Unless we attach a curious kind of semantic significance to the notion of personal identity, the abstraction we arrive at by generalizing over one speaker's utterances is, from the point of view of the radical interpreter, no more nor less significant than the ill-defined abstraction we call English. And to suggest that an idiolect is simply the language spoken by one person at one particular time, and so no abstraction at all, is just to say that what a speaker speaks is not a language, nor even any one idiolect, but a *series* of unique idiolects. And this is to admit that we have not found a way to describe in terms of semantically significant linguistic regularities the knowledge a speaker uses when successfully communicating. And we never will find a way to describe this knowledge in those terms, because it is not the mastery of a shared abstract structure of linguistic regularities, such as a language, that permits communication. What enables us to communicate is the mastery of something like an art, namely the art of theory construction, in the form of interpretation.

Clearly, no one is challenging the idea that English speakers use words in similar ways. This is a convenience which greatly facilitates theory formation. But it is not in principle a necessary, or sufficient, condition for communication to succeed. Accordingly, Davidson concludes that semantics has no use for the concept of a language.

He draws this conclusion, however, in part on the basis of a premise he shares with Dummett. This common premise is implicit in the articulation of their disagreement about the role of conventions in semantics. It is the notion that if the concept of a language has any theoretically interesting content, it must derive from a rationalization of linguistic competence. So, from the undeniable fact that natural languages are convention bound, Dummett concludes that linguistic meaning is essentially conventional. He concludes this, because he believes that what allows a speaker to be understood is the fact that the interpreter knows the speaker's language. The crucial piece of semantic knowledge must therefore be the knowledge of a language. And a language as an existing pattern, whether it is the Queen's English or Mrs Malaprop's peculiar version of it, is distinguished from other such patterns precisely by the fact that it embodies conventions that are different from those of other languages. Hence, for Dummett, linguistic competence *is* a knowledge of conventions.

Davidson agrees with Dummett that a natural language, if it is anything at all, is an existing pattern. And he agrees, importantly, that a language, if it is to be of any interest to the semanticist, must be that by which a particular population (the speakers of the language) are able to communicate. But, he argues, while there may well exist the kinds of regularity of language that Dummett claims are the conventions of meaning, it is *not* by virtue of her knowledge of these regularities that an interpreter is able to understand the meaning of what a speaker says. It is *because* he agrees with Dummett on the earlier point that Davidson goes on to infer that there is nothing for a language to be. All that is needed is the added premise that communication does not, as the radical-interpretation model shows, presuppose convention.

I suggest we drop the shared premise of these conflicting inferences. That way, we can without contradiction claim *both* that languages are convention-governed social practices *and* that a theory of meaning conceived as a rationalization of a speaker's linguistic competence does not involve the knowledge of conventions. I suggest, in other words, that whether we understand what someone says and whether we know what language is being spoken, are theoretically independent questions.

What do we gain by this divorce? To see that, we must first make explicit the fundamental assumption on which this separation appears unthinkable.

In practice, the questions of whether we understand the literal meaning of an utterance and whether we know the language employed are wholly interdependent. This is because interpretation normally proceeds by way of the kind of theoretical shortcuts I mentioned in connection with my criticism of Wallace in chapter 6, short cuts which are *ex hypothesi* unavailable to the radical interpreter. These short cuts can include a host of beliefs (psychological, biological, sociological, historical, etc.), beliefs that we rely on in our routine performances of the not-so-radical interpretation that is required, for instance, every time we clue in to the topic of some conversation. But most commonly, these short cuts are just the conventions of a language. We rely on these to such an extent that both Dummett and Hacking accuse Davidson of misrepresenting matters — either what actually goes on when speakers of the same language speak to and understand one another, or the meaning of 'interpretation' — when he claims that the radical-interpretation model is a model of all linguistic communication, domestic as well as foreign.[2]

As I will show, there is more than a semantic quibble here. While this disagreement appears to turn on nothing more than how to use the word 'interpretation', it in fact arises from a fundamental difference between the explanatory strategies at work. It is this difference I want to bring out.

We do not, Dummett' and Hacking agree, *interpret* domestic utterances. This is true, in so far as we do not very often go about as field linguists collecting the truth-conditions of the utterances of our neighbours in order to construct a theory of truth for their language. That is to say, we usually approach communicative encounters with some prior theory (or, as is more likely, a set of intersecting, not clearly defined alternative theories), and in most cases the prior theory turns out to be extremely handy as part of the basis for the construction of passing theories. We never start from scratch.

As an objection to the application of the concept of radical interpretation on the home scene, this has no force whatsoever. It appears to have force only so long as we question-beggingly insist that the concept of a language is that by which linguistic competence must be explicated. Because, so long as we think that knowing a language (as opposed to using language) is what makes linguistic communication possible, we will think of knowing a language as logically prior to the activity of interpretation. For Dummett and Hacking, to interpret an utterance is to render it in your own idiolect; what already *is* expressed in your own idiolect is not interpreted, you somehow just get it.[3] Further, on this view, even if we can give an account of interpretation, this appears to leave unanswered the question of what it *is* to have a language or idiolect, which is the very question semantics is supposed to answer. Accordingly, for Dummett, the radical-interpretation model is deeply unsatisfactory; it seems to take for granted the very competence it is supposed to illuminate.

This, however, is a misconception. It looks to Dummett as if the radical-interpretation model smuggles in the essential competence at the ground level by making it a requirement that the interpreter already has mastered a language. But this is not what it entails. On the contrary, it is a rejection of the very idea that the game we are after can be described as the mastery of a language. The crucial significance of the radical-interpretation model of linguistic communication lies in the fact that it reverses the logical priority of the concept of a language and the concept of interpretation. And this reversal finally works itself out in Davidson's writings as the rejection of the concept of a language as a theoretical tool.

The meanings or truth-conditions of sentences of a natural language may well be assumed in most contexts to be conventionally given (to have what Dummett calls 'a standard use'), and so understood without noticeable mental hesitation on the part of the interpreter. But this is no reason to restrict the use of 'interpretation' to cases where we ponder the meaning of what is said, giving it perhaps a non-literal meaning. All interpretation lies somewhere on a spectrum between what asymptotically approaches homophonic interpretation and what we might call absolute translation (that is, radical translation as Quine conceived of it). Unless we fall back on the notion of a shared language as the source of semantic power, there is no way to draw a line between interpreting an utterance and simply getting the meaning of it. Nor do we − and this is the crux of the matter − have reason to want to draw this line unless we think we need the notion of a shared language to explain communication. This is the assumption the radical-interpretation model denies, by postulating interpretation, not the mastery of a language, as what must be illuminated.

We have in the past proceeded on the assumption that to understand 'meaning', to understand what it is to understand what something means, we must give an account of what it is to know a language. Taking radical interpretation seriously entails that the only way to give content to the concept of a language is to show that there are shared features of strategies of interpretation. In this way, the concept of a language derives its content from our theory of interpretation, not vice versa. No matter how conventional our use of language, the only way to *theoretically specify* what the sentences of a natural language mean is to construct a theory of truth. And to this end, neither conventions nor shared languages makes any contribution.

There is, however, no denying the need for a concept of a convention-governed practice to explain such things as our propensity to correct ourselves when made aware of having misused some expression, even in cases where we are actually understood. We rely on such a body of conventions not just when correcting errors, but also, for example, when we lie. But to point out this fact is not to argue against Davidson. His claim is that what I described above as the shared features of strategies of interpretation have no *semantic* significance. They are heuristic devices, on Davidson's view, that do not come into play when we attempt to describe what it is an interpreter knows in virtue of which she understands the meaning of an utterance.

However, in dismissing the body of conventions that constitute a language as a contingent feature of linguistic communication, as nothing more than a complex, and immensely valuable, practical aid, Davidson obscures the dialectical relation between meaning and what we might call the production of meaning. Meaning, understanding the meaning of an utterance, is what is modelled in radical interpretation. The production of meaning, on the other hand, is modelled by what we call a language. By divorcing the concept of a language from that of linguistic competence, as I have suggested, we recover the possibility of exploring a semantically significant relation between interpretation and bodies of conventions. This possibility is precluded both by those who, like Dummett, take linguistic competence to be the mastery of a language, and by those who would follow Davidson in regarding conventions as semantically irrelevant. The middle way allows us, in effect, to reinstate the concept of a language as theoretically significant, without giving up the primacy of interpretation.

In practice, what governs our use of expressions are the conventions of our language. What are these conventions? As strategic short cuts of interpretation, they are, among other things, the conventional determinations of the truth-conditions of sentences.

We do not, usually, consciously ponder the literal meaning of assertions made in our own language. But if we want to make theoretically explicit the meaning of sentences of our own language — if we ask how we know we are speaking the same language — then radical interpretation (leaning toward the homophonic) comes into play. Still, in a normal speech situation, this will not happen, for here conventional strategies, not the constructing of a truth-theory, determine what truth-conditions we attach to utterances. The point is this: in so far as we are speakers of a language, the truth-conditions of the sentences of that language are conventionally taken for granted. But linguistic meaning does *not* essentially involve conventions. There is, then, no reason to suppose a priori that the conventionally attached truth-conditions of sentences of a language and the truth-theoretically determined truth-conditions of the assertions that speakers make, necessarily coincide. That is to say, a discrepancy between the radical interpretation of meaning and the conventional production of meaning is at least conceivable.

To see that there is an issue of semantics here, it is essential to think of linguistic communication as an ongoing, dynamic process. It is the fact that language is not static, that interpretation is modelled by the continuous creation of truth-theories and not by the knowledge of any one truth-theory, that allows a discrepancy between convention and truth-theory to appear. The reason is that while a truth-theory is a synchronic generalization, a body of conventions represents a diachronic generalization. Changes in usage will be reflected differently in the two kinds of theoretical structures.

To see what the foregoing means, let us look at the production of meaning through the body of conventions we call a language. The individual speaker stands in the same relation to the conventions of his/her language as Aristotle's *phronimos* does to the virtues, or rather to 'that principle by which the man of practical wisdom would determine [virtue]' (*Nicomachean Ethics*, 1006b36). A virtue is defined with respect to the hermeneutic circle running through the rational principle or abstract moral precept — the major premise of Aristotle's practical syllogism — and the concrete actions of the *phronimos* — the conclusions of the syllogism. Similarly, every application of a linguistic convention, every instance of conforming to it, is also an interpretation and specification of that convention. If it is a convention to use "snow is white" to say that snow is white, this convention is hammered out only in a series of assertions that snow is white, in just the way the meaning of a moral precept is hammered out for Aristotle in the actions of the *phronimos*.

What is significant here is that while radical interpretation is completely fluid in its ascription of semantic significance to words, and instantaneously absorbs any change in the truth-theoretic significance of a word by producing a revised truth-theory, this is not true of the conventions that govern our use of words and sentences. Conventions, being hammered out over time, are of varying viscosity. For this reason, changes in use have a gradual impact on conventions, but an immediate impact on the radical interpreter. In so far as we in practice communicate as speakers of a language, that is, by relying on conventions, and not as radical interpreters, the potential lag between the convention-bound use of language and the radical interpretation of language represents a possible diffusion of meaning, a blurring of linguistic understanding. To speak a language, in other words, is necessarily always to be in danger of misinterpreting what is said.

What is the theoretical significance of this? Is it not just a precious way of stating the obvious fact that radical interpretation is an *idealization* of linguistic competence, an idealization on which meaning is much sharper than it ever is to any real language user? If there were nothing more to say about the discrepancy between the radical interpretation of meaning and the conventional production of meaning, this would be true. But, in fact, there *is* more to say, as I will show in the following chapter. We can give accounts of the ways in which convention-changes, changes in the social practice that is a language, affect our linguistic understanding. More precisely, we can give accounts of the specific nature of certain discrepancies, we can explain their genesis, and we can show in what ways they blur or distort the meaning of our discourse. This kind of analysis, which connects semantics with a field of inquiry spanning the critique of ideology, the sociology of knowledge and the history of science, hinges on our keeping the concepts of linguistic competence and of speaking a language apart. Only then can we conceive of the possibility of slippage between diachronically determined linguistic conventions and the synchronic truth-theories of radical interpretation. This idea provides us, as we will see, with a general framework for understanding the various manifestations — in science, in ethics, in politics — of the conceptually troublesome phenomenon of incommensurability.

NOTES

1 Lewis's book *Convention* (Lewis, 1969) has become the measure of any account of the concept, and his analysis (for which see also Lewis, 1975) is usually the starting point of discussion even for those who have serious doubts about its adequacy. It is, fortunately, irrelevant to the points I will be making in the present chapter whether or not Lewis's analysis is correct in all details. I will assume that something much like it is needed to make the distinction between conventions and other kinds of regularities displayed in our behaviour.

2 For Hacking's objections to Davidson's use of 'interpretation', see Hacking (1986, pp. 450–1), for Dummett's, see Dummett (1986, p. 464).

3 Dummett refers to Wittgenstein's analysis of rule following, and claims that there is, similarly, 'a way of understanding a sentence or an utterance that does not consist in putting an interpretation on it' (Dummett, 1986, p. 464).

9
What is Incommensurability?

In 1962, Thomas S. Kuhn published *The Structure of Scientific Revolutions* to instant notoriety. Since then, the concept of incommensurability has been a focal point of debates about the nature of rationality.[1] One recurring theme in the many and varied discussions is the notion that there is something semantically suspect about the idea of incommensurability. This has been the main thrust of much anti-Kuhnian polemic, though the argument takes different forms. So, for instance, in the years following the publication of Kuhn's book, prominent theorists of science like Karl Popper, Israel Scheffler and Dudley Shapere all responded to Kuhn's theory of scientific development with some version of the claim that Kuhn had no adequate theory of meaning.[2] If he had, the implication was, he would not have said what he did about the incommensurability of scientific paradigms. This perception has remained predominant in many quarters; Hilary Putnam, for example, implied not very long ago that to account for the history of science in terms of incommensurability is semantically incoherent (see Putnam, 1981, p. 115). And as recently as 1985, Michael Devitt found it necessary to devote a section of his book *Realism and Truth* to dismiss the idea of incommensurability (see Devitt, 1985, pp. 151–5).

In the social sciences, an interestingly similar debate followed the publication of Peter Winch's monograph *The Idea of a Social Science and its Relation to Philosophy* (1958).[3] Winch, steeped in the thinking of the later Wittgenstein and working in the tradition of the hermeneutic concept of *verstehen*, argued that to understand an alien culture it was necessary to understand it somehow from within, on its own terms and by its own standards. And he was talking not just about moral standards but about cognitive standards.

Winch, like Kuhn, was criticized from different angles, but a common response was the purported *reductio* that if Winch were correct, cross-cultural understanding would not be possible at all.

What Winch's critics, like Kuhn's, reacted to was the idea of a framework of understanding, of a conceptual scheme, that could only be properly appraised from the inside. This, it seemed, led inescapably to relativism and, ultimately, to solipsism.

While it is not my primary purpose here to review either Kuhn and his critics or Winch and the rationality theorists, the argument of the present chapter bears directly on these debates. By providing an analysis of the semantics of incommensurability, I will show that there is no relation between incommensurability, on the one hand, and intranslatability and relativism, on the other.

In spite of such historically erudite and conceptually fine-grained analyses as those provided by Rorty and Richard Bernstein, of carefully detailed readings of Kuhn like Gerald Doppelt's and of the fact that much of what Kuhn and Winch said is now taken for granted even by their critics, we do not have any clear theoretical conception of what incommensurability is.[4] That the concept remains murky is attested to by the fact that some philosophers still dismiss it on a priori grounds. Putnam provides an example. In a chapter of *Reason, Truth, and History* entitled 'Two Conceptions of Rationality' he gives the following definition: 'The incommensurability thesis is the thesis that terms used in another culture, say, the term "temperature" as used by a seventeenth-century scientist, cannot be equated in meaning or reference with any terms or expressions *we* posses' (Putnam, 1981, p. 114). Putnam attributes this thesis to the Paul Feyerabend of *Against Method* (1978) and to the Kuhn of *The Structure of Scientific Revolutions* (1970) and subsequent papers.[5] It is, according to Putnam, a self-refuting thesis, because 'if this thesis were really true then we could not translate other languages – or even past stages of our own language – at all. And if we cannot interpret organisms' noises at all, them we have no grounds for regarding them as *thinkers*, *speakers*, or even *persons'* (Putnam, 1981, p. 114). Presented with this neat little argument, one wonders how anyone ever could have thought that incommensurability was anything to worry (or rejoice) about, how anyone ever could have failed to see that to 'tell us that Galileo had "incommensurable" notions *and then to go on to describe them at length* is totally incoherent' (Putnam, 1981, p. 115). If this were all there is to it, the hazy idea that our communicative understanding under certain conditions may be fogged by an incommensurability of concepts and descriptions would seem to evaporate with the first rays of analysis.

This is *not* all there is to it, though, as Devitt's recent attack on incommensurability brings out in an interesting way. Devitt writes: 'Incommensurability is the thesis that because of Meaning, Reference and Ontological Change, theories T and T′ in the one area are semantically incomparable ...' (Devitt, 1985, p. 151). He speaks of 'semantic incomparability' in order to clearly distinguish the semantic nature of the thesis from neighbouring epistemological questions, and takes the notion to entail that there is no common language, neither the languages of T or T′ nor any other, in which both theories can be rendered. Devitt, then, like Puntnam, takes it that incommensurability implies intranslatability. And thus understood, claims Devitt, the incommensurability thesis is false (Devitt, 1985, p. 155). Note, however, that Devitt does not argue that the notion is incoherent, nor that the thesis is self-contradictory. The important difference between Devitt and earlier critics of Kuhn, such as Popper, Shapere and Scheffler – or Putnam – is that Devitt does not provide an alleged *reductio* of the concept of incommensurability, he does not give anything like an a priori argument.

As Devitt points out, what is presumed to make the theories T and T′ in the same area – say, physics – incommensurable is the fact that switching from one theory to the other involves changes in the semantic values of the terms and expressions of the theories. In Devitt's parlance, that is to say that the terms of the theories are not co-referential. The theories postulate different ontologies. According to Devitt, incommensurability theorists like Kuhn take this change to imply the impossibility of semantically comparing the content of the theories, and so also of criticizing or refuting one theory using the terms of the other (see Devitt, 1985, p. 151).

Against this position, Devitt argues that changes in the semantic value of terms from one theory to another do *not* imply that the theories cannot be compared. Invoking what he calls quasi-logical relations based on the concept of partial co-reference, he claims that 'Reference Change alone is not sufficient for incomparability' (Devitt, 1985, p. 153). The idea is straightforward: theory T' may make a distinction that theory T does not make, so that, for example, one T-term is applied to two separate T'-phenomena. For instance, to borrow Devitt's example, using the language of relativity theory, we can say that the Newtonian term 'mass' 'partially referred to both relativistic and proper mass' (Devitt, 1985, pp. 153—4). But the fact that reference changes in this way from one theory to the next does not in any way preclude normative comparison of the theories. It requires only that we work out the relations of partial reference between the two theories. It is, Devitt argues, only through the distorting lens of a description theory of reference that changes in semantic values of expressions from one theory to another could be taken to imply that these theories are semantically incomparable.

What makes Devitt's line of attack interesting is that he does not deny the contentious doctrine of meaning-change. This doctrine — that the semantic values of expressions can change between paradigms — is precisely the target of the objections put forth by earlier critics; Putnam, for one, explicitly equates the incomensurability thesis with the doctrine of meaning-change (see the quotation on p. 115). Yet what clearly follows from Devitt's argument is that semantic change does not necessarily imply semantic incomparability. In taking this position, Devitt, it appears, is not lining up with the earlier critics of Kuhn, as he apparently takes himself to be doing. For the claim that incommensurability is intranslatability (semantic incomparability) is not, as we shall see, advanced by Kuhn. On the contrary, that the doctrine of meaning-change implies that the languages of different theories are semantically incomparable has been an essential premise in the various alleged *reductios* of the notion of incommensurability put forth over the years. What Devitt has done is to show that this premise does not hold.

With Devitt's polemic, the analysis of incommensurability in terms of a reference-based semantics has come full circle: on a description-theory of reference it appears that meaning-change leads to intranslatability, and this supposed implication was seen as a *reductio* of the notion; it was seen as demonstrating that the doctrine of meaning-change must be false, on pain of making communication impossible. Devitt's argument is very different: he assumes at the outset the identification of incommensurability with semantic incomparability and then uses the notion of partial reference to show that the doctrine of meaning change does not imply intranslatability. Devitt concludes from this that the incommensurability thesis is false. What he has actually done is to undermine the previous arguments against it.

What we can learn from Devitt's argument (apart from the fact that the expressions in the incommensurability debate appear to be semantically unstable) is that the fundamental issue in this debate should not be *whether* the meaning of basic terms can change in the course of scientific (and other) revolutions. The real — and tangled — issue is the *nature* and the *degree* of the semantic changes and discrepancies that can be conceptually allowed. And on this issue, Devitt and Kuhn are clearly divided. For Kuhn, the semantic changes brought about in the course of a scientific revolution can in principle be radical, and his choice of metaphors indicate that he thinks they often are. For Devitt, on the other hand, the degree of semantic change that can be absorbed is constrained by what can be limned by the logical apparatus of partial reference, which presupposes a significant degree of continuity in the postulated ontology from one theory or paradigm to another.

Devitt can allow a degree of semantic change without precluding semantic comparison because he is committed to a theory of reference which is more sophisticated than the description theory. But the conceptual tension between semantic change and semantic comparability remains. For Devitt, too, translatability is preserved only through the continuity of reference, albeit in a more subtle manner than earlier critics of Kuhn supposed. And seen in this perspective, Devitt's position is solidly anchored within the traditional, reference-based opposition to Kuhn and the other 'radicals', as indeed Devitt himself takes it to be.

At the core of the incommensurability debate, then, is the question of whether continuity of reference is what makes communication possible. Whatever else we might say about the incommensurability thesis, it is clearly intended to deny that this is so. A semantic account of incommesurability would consequently have to be framed in terms of a conception of semantics which does not make essential use of reference. Davidson, of course, provides us with just such a conception.

Assimilating the concept of incommensurability to a Davidsonian semantics, however, would appear to be highly problematic. For the incommensurability thesis is not only a denial of the view that continuity of reference is a necessary presumption of successful communication. It is also, perhaps primarily, intended to positively identify a certain kind of semantic obstruction between would-be communicators – a semantic obstruction which, as I have suggested, is commonly taken by critics of the idea to be intranslatability. And on the radical-interpretation model of semantics, it is hard to conceive of any such semantic obstruction. It is so hard, in fact, that the radical-interpretation model is generally presumed to yield a powerful argument against the very idea of incommensurability.

This argument, echoed by Putnam's perfunctory dismissal of Kuhn and Feyerabend, was famously provided by Davidson in his Presidential Address to the Eastern Division Meeting of the American Philosophical Association in 1973. In 'On the Very Idea of a Conceptual Scheme' (*Inquiries*, pp. 183–98) Davidson takes on the idea of incommensurability understood, in the usual fashion, as intranslatability. The analysis provided in this article shows that if incommensurability is to have any place within a Davidsonian conception of semantics, we cannot interpret it in terms of intranslatability. But it is essential that we are clear as to why we cannot make this identification, and as to exactly what Davidson's argument against the idea of intranslatability does and does not entail.

In 'On the Very Idea of a Conceptual Scheme' Davidson equates a conceptual scheme with a language or a set of intertranslatable languages, and then goes on to show that the only such set we can conceive of is the set of all possible languages. But he is *not* arguing to the Kantian conclusion that we all (fortunately) share the same conceptual scheme. No substantive conclusions about similarities of dissimilarities between various ways of carving up the world follow from Davidson's reasoning. The real point of 'On the Very Idea of a Conceptual Scheme' is simply that if we are extenionalists about meaning, we cannot imagine what it is for a language to have an 'inside', one that remains inaccessible to us even if we have somehow managed to map the 'outside' of the language by the pairing off of extensions of sentences in radical interpretation. And this means that we cannot make sense of the idea of intranslatable languages.

Incommensurability understood as intranslatability is not conceivable from the point of view of an extensional semantics. Why is this so? To see this, it is necessary to distinguish intranslatability from practical difficulties of translation. Radical translation may proceed awkwardly or slowly, the interpreter may have difficulty finding any patterns on which to base her hypothetical T-sentences, she may have difficulty narrowing down the choice between several rudimentary theories, etc. But even the most bizarre discourse is in principle accessible to her. If she hangs around long enough, is sufficiently observant, and combines a remarkable memory with an equally remarkable flexibility of mind, there is no reason, in principle, why she should not come to understand even a group of speakers who on any given day are concerned solely, say, with what happened two days earlier. And as long as there is no reason *in principle* why she should not come to understand what is being said, we are not entitled to speak of intranslatability.

Intranslatability would exist only if either an interpreter were in principle unable to form any kind of truth-theory, or if any workable truth-theory she were to produce necessarily failed to capture the meaning of what was said, and so necessarily had to be wrong. The latter clearly hinges on the possibility of giving content to the concept of meaning without relying on the concept of truth, and hence warrants no further examination in the present context. What about the former? Could we not speak of incommensurability in those cases where radical interpretation simply did not work?

In a defence of what has become known as the strong thesis of the sociology of science (Hesse, 1980), Mary Hesse imagines an example intended to show that translatability cannot be a criterion of languagehood. Suppose, she suggests, that a group of people 'talked only about more important things like their relation to the spirit world, and not all about the mundane process of keeping alive, procreation, and so on' (Hesse, 1980, p. 40). How could a radical interpreter of our secular culture ever hope to understand this language? It would appear that while the interpreter has no access to the meaning of what is being said, she has no warrant for concluding that her spiritual subjects do not have a language.

The problem with this thought experiment is that if there are no observable correlations between the sounds these people make and observable features of the world they live in, then it is impossible to see how any of them ever came to learn their *own* language. If there are such correlations, that is, if meaning does make an empirical difference, then these correlations must be accessible to the interpreter as well. While they may not be the kinds of empirical observables that the interpreter is used to look for, this fact – no doubt explicable largely in sociological and anthropological terms – only makes translation difficult, not impossible. Perhaps, though, one might object, it so happened that while it appears that the speakers are talking about observ- ables, they actually take themselves to be discussing the spirit world. Furthermore, one might claim, this might be so even if the interpreter after much effort and with great hermeneutic zeal produces an ideal theory which appears to fit the available evidence very nicely. We just cannot know. But to say this would merely be to insist that meaning is irreducibly intensional, and so to beg the question at issue: it would constitute a retreat, from the claim that there are certain cases when we are in principle unable to radically translate, to the more fundamental claim that the radical- translation model of linguistic communication is false. As a de- fence of the idea of intranslatability, it is therefore useless unless it is made against the back-drop of an alternative theory of meaning.

In general, it is always possible to form some theory, although not, perhaps, one sufficiently unique to be very useful. The evi- dence might be very slim, as in the case of Linear B referred to in chapter 6, but in these sorts of cases the problem is not the impossibility of forming theories. The problem here lies in insuf- ficient opportunity to test our hypotheses, which leaves us unable to eliminate a sufficiently large number of possible theories to make much headway. But then there is no intrinsic feature of the languages spoken that precludes communication.

We can, if we like, interpret all kinds of things as speaking. We obey signals of all sorts all the time. Some of us frequently subject our pets to radical interpretation, some of us find out about past and coming events from the entrails of feathered bipeds, some of us discover our personal strengths and weaknesses by plotting the relative positions of large objects in space. We could even, as Douglas Hofstadter suggests (Hofstadter and Dennett, 1982), talk to ant-hills, or at least regard them as speaking to us. It is a sufficient condition for radical interpretation that we are able to correlate some identifiable complex state of our chosen subject with some identifiable state of the world. Incommensurability understood as the impossibility of forming a theory of truth by radical interpretation is not therefore a question of a relation among languages at all. Those hypothetical cases imagined by theorists to be cases of intranslatable languages are better construed as cases where the would-be interpreter faces conflicting evidence. On the one hand, she may have evidence of some kind that a unique, relatively fine-grained truth-theory is applicable to the noises (or movements, or whatever) her subjects make; on the other, she may have evidence that it is not. The former kind of evidence would probably be the sort of thing that tempts us to attempt interpretation, such as the fact that the subjects appear to be a lot like the interpreter in what she happens to regard as significant respects. The latter kind of evidence would be her failure to discern any kind of pattern, or a sufficiently unique pattern, in what she thought was linguistic activity. Obviously, since neither kind of evidence is ever conclusive, there is no contradiction here, no need to postulate intranslatable languages. It is worth pointing out, too, that cases where conflicting evidence of this kind appears to be finely balanced are much harder to imagine than some theorists appear to believe. The reason is that one of the primary incentives to attempt interpretation, one of the key factors in the awakening of our suspicion that we are dealing with language users, is precisely the recognition of patterns that can reasonably be taken to constitute linguistic behaviour. The difficulty lies in imagining the kind of evidence that convinces us that a given subject possesses and makes use of linguistic competence, evidence that is also compatible with our inability to detect any kind of pattern in the subject's presumed linguistic behaviour. What sort of evidence could this possibly be?

Clearly, in most cases the various indications we go by lend overwhelming support to one conclusion or the other — witness the agility with which we switch back and forth between a stance of linguistic interpretation and one of non-linguistic interpretation in response to changes in our environment. Indeed, a person lacking the ability to make this judgement swiftly and effectively would be regarded by most of us as insane.

However, it is not just because the idea of intranslatability presupposes a concept of meaning that works independently of the concept of truth that it is an unusable idea. An equally fundamental difficulty arises from the fact that the concept of intranslatability is indissolubly tied to a semantics of languages. The concept becomes impossible to explicate once we see the *process of interpretation* — rather than the mastery of linguistic structures — as the fundamental subject of semantic theory: intranslatability is supposed to describe a relation between languages, namely the relation between languages that possess some intrinsic characteristic in virtue of which it is impossible to translate one into the other.[6] But if my argument in the preceding chapter is sound, if we are only coincidentally speakers of languages, then it makes no sense at all to conceive of languages as having properties that preclude translation. Only if we think of the mastery of a language as the foundation of our linguistic capacity, and think of interpretation as an ability to be illuminated *via* the mastery of a language, is it conceivable that there may be something about the languages themselves that might in certain cases make translation, in principle, impossible.

It appears that we are left with a choice: either we follow Davidson, Devitt, Putnam, et al. and regard incommensurability as being or implying the intranslatability of languages, in which case we should dismiss it as a philosophical fiction, no matter where we stand on the issue of reference; or we come up with an alternative interpretation of incommensurability claims. If we choose the former, we should be very clear that we are taking a stand on an issue in the theory of meaning, and not in the ongoing debate about various kinds of relativism. Hesse is justified in her suspicion of a priori arguments about necessary translatability in the rationalist case against, for example, the symmetry thesis of

Barry Barnes and David Bloor.[7] But rather than engage in doomed attempts at constructing hypothetical cases of intranslatability, we should point out to the defenders of universal reason that the issue between them and the relativistic sociologists of knowledge simply does not turn on the possibility of translation. In their contributions to *Rationality and Relativism* (Hollis and Lukes, 1982), Martin Hollis, Lukes, Dan Sperber, William Newton-Smith and Ernest Gellner, all take the position that relativism is false because there must be some 'bridgehead' of common beliefs and standards uniting the interpreter and the interpreted. But just as the principle of charity has no implications about the similarities or dissimilarities of respective world views, so the ineliminable possibility of translation is no guarantee that we share criteria of truth or have a common core of empirical knowledge or that our languages enable us to refer to some fundamental common set of referents.

The reason is that the kind of translinguistic truth stipulated by Davidsonian semantics is entirely without epistemological ramifications, and so is not the kind of truth that cuts much anti-relativist ice. It is nothing but a point of contact between, or more innocuously, the coincidence of, what an interpreter observes and the utterances a subject makes. The semantic concept of truth, far from being extralinguistic, is a *product* of interpretation; there is nothing more to it than an interpreter's regarding as causally related a bit of presumed linguistic activity and some feature of the world.[8] There is no immutable relation in sight here, no special truth-indicating property for sentences to have, since such causal relations are subject to constant change. Nor – crucially – can these causal relations ever be used as epistemic supports, since they themselves are nothing but empirical hypotheses based on inductive generalizations.

It is a mistake to conceive of *criteria* of truth as something which interlocutors independently possess and which must coincide as a necessary condition of interpretation. Conversely, we cannot infer from the fact of translatability any set of criteria of truth, maxims of observation, or rules of inference that speakers of intertranslatable languages necessarily share. The idea of criteria of truth as something that individuals, societies, cultures, or species may or may not have in common is an idea that can only emerge in the *context* of interpretation. It is logically dependent on the success of interpretation, that is, on the application of the *semantic* concept of truth. This is true when we order groceries at the corner store and it is true when Evans-Pritchard inquires of his Azande informants about their beliefs concerning causality. While semantic truth is instantly applicable across the board, this is *not* because of any transcendentally necessary convergence in the criteria we rely on in judging sentences true or false. It could only occur to us to wonder about criteria of truth, our own or those of the Azande—or our grocer's—once we have begun to understand what is said. Linguistic Kantianism, the idea that there are a priori conditions of languagehood that guarantee that the world appears pretty much the same to everyone who talks, gets no support whatever from Davidson's argument against intranslatability. The belief that it does is the result of a familiar confusion of the semantic concept of truth and epistemological notions like justi-fication of beliefs and criteria of correctness. The point can be put thus: while there is nothing that can be said in one language that must remain ineffable in another, this is neither because of a happy conjunction of the sorts of things we say, nor because of a putative necessary similarity of logical structure between all pos-sible languages. It is only because of *what it is* to say something. Appreciation of this distinction ought to make anti-relativists less eager to make so much of the incoherence of the idea of in-translatability. The only form of relativism that necessarily goes by the board is the extreme form of linguistic relativism which contends that languages might stand in such a relation to one another that linguistic communication across the language barrier is in principle blocked. But not even the father of contemporary linguistic relativism, the true amateur Benjamin Lee Whorf, is reasonably read as claiming this.[9]

If the semantic obstruction implied by the idea of incommen-surability is not intranslatability, what then can it be? As both Rorty and Bernstein point out, Kuhn certainly did not mean to equate the two (see Rorty, 1979, pp. 302n., 315–16; Bernstein, 1983, pp. 79–86). Indeed, Kuhn makes it clear that what is required in cases of incommensurability is precisely interpretation or translation. In the *Postscript*, dated 1969, he says: 'Briefly put, what the participants in a communication break-down can do is recognize each other as members of different language-communities and then become translators' (Kuhn, 1970, p. 202). It seems odd, therefore, to attribute to Kuhn the idea that incommensurability implies intranslatability. Indeed, on one reading of Kuhn, the apparent issue of semantics is nothing but a red herring. Those who take this line, like Bernstein and Rorty, see the strongly critical reactions to Kuhn's work not as a reaction to a supposedly incoherent theory of meaning, but as a result of a commitment to a certain notion of rationality.

Critics like Shapere, Scheffler, Popper and Imre Lakatos who denounce Kuhn as a relativist or an irrationalist take a fixed conception of scientific rationality as a measure of Kuhn's account of science: since we cannot, as Kuhn sees it, rely on any pre-determined method or decision procedure to provide an objective decision in cases of paradigm conflict, science according to Kuhn is irrational. And since these critics regard science as paradigmatically rational, they conclude that Kuhn's account must be wrong.

Defending Kuhn against these charges, Rorty and Bernstein take him to be discussing not whether science is rational, but the nature of scientific rationality. So Bernstein says: 'Kuhn (and others) ... have not shown that science is *irrational*, but rather that something is fundamentally wrong with the idea that commensurability is the essence of scientific rationality' (Bernstein, 1983, p. 86). This reading of Kuhn is central to the move away from what Lakatos labelled 'instant rationality' (see Lakatos, 1970).[10] The key element of this move is perhaps the conception of principles of rationality, rules of inference, laws of reason, etc., not as rules but as values. As values, they have a social, historical existence, and they are the subjects of commitment, argument and interpretation. This conception of scientific rationality brings it, as particularly Bernstein emphasizes, into close alignment with Aristotle's *phronesis*.

Reading Kuhn's work in this way, as a critique of the concept of rationality, allows us also to make interesting sense of his notion of paradigm. As the frameworks of normal science, the entities between which a putative relation of incommensurability is supposed to exist, paradigms are the conceptual cornerstone of Kuhn's model of scientific development. Notoriously, the concept is far from univocal.[11]

I shall follow a suggestion made by Jack Carloye, and regard a paradigm not as a particular achievement, a particular group of problems, or an abstract set of cognitive values, but as a particular practice (see Carloye, 1985). As a social practice, it is constituted by the commitment to some cluster of values, and this commitment manifests itself in general adherence to a certain set of conventions. A paradigm in this sense embodies a particular historical narrative, namely the formation, interpretation and specification of those conventions of reasoning and language that are the distinguishing features of the paradigm. Understood in this way, the concept of a paradigm is something very much like Hans-Georg Gadamer's notion of a tradition.[12]

Taking a paradigm to be a social practice, governed by the conventions that embody a particular cluster of cognitive values, we can understand incommensurability as a matter of a divergence of cognitive value. Clearly, no effective decision procedure can be agreed upon by people who cannot agree upon the criteria, or upon the relative ranking of the criteria, of what constitutes a rational decision. Such a divergence would make commensuration impossible, in the sense that it would preclude, as Rorty puts it, the application of 'a set of rules which will tell us how rational agreement can be reached on what would settle the issue on every point where statements seem to conflict' (Rorty, 1979, p. 316).

Yet these divergent cognitive values are themselves open to discussion. And such discussion can certainly be rational, even if no predetermined algorithm can be found. Perhaps the best account we have of such non-criterial rationality (to borrow Putnam's term), is Aristotle's account of *phronesis*.[13] Cross-paradigmatic argument—what Gadamer describes as a fusion of horizons (see Gadamer, 1975, e.g. pp. 269–70)—then becomes a matter of wisdom, in the Aristotelian sense. It becomes a matter of judgement which is not the application of a given standard as much as it is an interpretation, a hammering out, of standards. But Aristotle's *phronimos* was an individual (albeit an ideal) whose practical reason provided an instant measure of moral standards. The (re)-interpretation and specification of cognitive values that goes on in what Rorty calls abnormal discourse, is a supra-individual, communally constituted process, which can only be rationally reconstructed retrospectively in the light presently thrown by our continuously evolving standards.[14]

The relation of incommensurability is ultimately what distinguishes Kuhn's account of the history of science from the linear, cumulative conception he was criticizing. As the mediation of cumulative progress and mere change, incommensurability is the springboard of Kuhn's *aufhebung*, the bounce in the dialectic of the evolution of science. But while Kuhn insists that we certainly can and do make normative, comparative, rational judgements about incommensurable paradigms, he also stresses that incommensurability represents a communication breakdown. He never retreats from the position that scientists working in incommensurable paradigms actually use words differently. As we have seen, it is this latter claim — that a paradigm shift represents a change in the meaning of the scientific vocabulary — that is the focal point of arguments accusing Kuhn of cognitive relativism: If there is disagreement not just about *which* criteria are relevant to the rational resolution of conflicts, but about the *meaning* of those criteria, it is impossible for scientists working in different paradigms even to understand each other.

Construing paradigms as practices governed by historically specified conventions, and relying on a hermeneutic model for the rationality of cross-paradigmatic discourse, it appears that the criticism levelled against Kuhn by those who charge him with leaving scientists trapped within mutually impenetrable frameworks can be deflected. But, in claiming that the charge of relativism and irrationalism is directed at a straw man, we take on the responsibility of giving an interpretation of incommensurability that preserves what was exciting and provocative in Kuhn's theory. The problem we then face is that while Kuhn himself explicitly denies that incommensurability implies intranslatability, it is not easy to see how the purported relation of incommensurability between Kuhnian paradigms will do the conceptual work Kuhn himself requires of it, unless we take it to intend something precariously close to intranslatability.

The question is: How can we maintain Kuhn's thesis that incommensurability implies a change in the meaning of the words of our vocabulary without falling prey to the *reductio* that this would exclude rational communication?

Sympathetic commentators like Bernstein and Rorty de-emphasize Kuhn's more problematic semantic claims, attempting to bring them into line with Kuhn's explicitly held view that cross-paradigmatic argument can be rational. Rorty, for example, chooses explicitly to dispense with the idea that 'commensurable' is to be construed as 'assigning the same meaning to terms'. He says:

> This sense – which is the one often used in discussing Kuhn – does not seem to me a useful one, given the fragility of the notion of 'sameness of meaning.' To say that parties to a controversy 'use terms in different ways' seems to me an unenlightening way of describing the fact that they cannot find a way of agreeing on what would settle the issue. (Rorty, 1979, p. 316)

For Rorty, there is therefore no problem of semantics in the area, since there is no reason to suppose that an account of this sort of meta-disagreement, or divergence of cognitive value, should be given in semantic rather than in sociological or historical terms. Indeed, it would appear that an explanation necessarily would have to be couched in historical terms.

While insisting on this last point, I will argue that incommensurability does have semantic import, and that we no longer need to dodge the semantic issue in the way Rorty proposes. We can give an account incorporating Kuhn's claim that incommensurability is a matter of meaning-change by construing incommensurability as part of the semantic evolution of a language. In this way we can agree with Kuhn's critics – and, presumably, with Kuhn himself – that incommensurability is primarily a semantic notion, while insisting with his defenders that it is also a coherent one. We can, in other words, give content to the idea of a semantic obstruction other than intranslatability. This allows us to retain the idea, given up by Rorty but surely held by Kuhn, that talk of meaning-change is not just an unenlightening way of pointing out a communicative failure, but actually a way of *explaining* that failure.

To see this, we need to return to the central point of the preceding chapter, chapter 8. There I distinguished between meaning or linguistic understanding as modelled by radical translation, and the production of meaning, as modelled by a conventionally constituted existing structure or social practice, that is, by a language.

Radical interpretation, as we saw, is a matter of formulating series of synchronic truth-theories, whereas the conventions of a language are diachronic generalizations of linguistic practice. Such linguistic conventions, I suggested, are of varying viscosity, and for all practical purposes our communication is bound by them. We rely on conventions to understand and make ourselves understood. Incommensurability, as a communication breakdown, can be understood as a breakdown of linguistic conventions, caused by changes in use that are too abrupt to be absorbed smoothly, or changes that a particular set of conventions are too rigid to accommodate. Semantically, then, incommensurability is a disruption in the ongoing interpretation-through-application of our linguistic conventions.

There is perhaps little that is new in this claim, taken by itself. What is new is that we do not have to construe this breakdown of conventions as implying intranslatability. Putnam's *reductio* can be blocked, because while a breakdown of linguistic conventions signal some change or other in the meaning of what is said, this change is not intractable. Since only the production of meaning *via* language, and *not* linguistic meaning itself, is conventionally constituted, the meaning of what is said is in principle *theoretically recoverable*, even though the conventions of linguistic communication are changing.

That linguistic conventions change, for example in the course of the history of science, is something that becomes apparent when would-be interlocutors find themselves engaged in incommensurable discourse, in which conflicts appear irresolvable because there is no shared conception of what is to count as a resolution. In incommensurable discourse, participants who take themselves to be speaking the same language, actually are not. We might say that they are not interlocutors, because what they say – their locutions – cannot pass between them. This way of putting matters appears to construct a barrier against the possibility of communication only if we think that 'speaking the same language' is what makes linguistic understanding possible. That this is so has simply been taken for granted by those who think the concept of incommensurability incoherent. But in chapter 8, we saw that this premise is defeasible. The meaning of a sentence depends not on any set of conventions, but on the theory of truth which produces the appropriate T-sentence. Incommensurability is a disruption in the conventional *production* of meaning, not a disintegration of meaning. Incommensurability in discourse leaves us in a situation where we can no longer rely on our language, the set of conventions whereby we normally effect understanding, to secure linguistic communication. But this does not imply that communication is not possible, only that *interpretation*, rather than reliance on convention, is required to a greater degree than is usual.

It might seem as if I am leaving out cases of incommensurability where the problem is not a divergence or disruption in a structure of linguistic conventions, but a failure to achieve the convergence of quite separate, independently generated and existing traditions or paradigms. While I am able to account for, for example, Kuhnian incommensurability, it might be objected that I cannot accommodate the incommensurability of, say, Western science and Azande magic.

While it is true, however, that my construal of incommensurability does not permit us to speak of relations of incommensurability between independently existing linguistic structures or evolving traditions, this is hardly an objection to the analysis. The reason is that the objection *presupposes* that failure of convergence marks an encounter between intranslatable languages. Certainly, if Azande magicians and Western physicists were to discuss causality, incommensurability would *arise*. But it would arise because translation would too often be *wrong*, which is to say that the interlocutors would frequently believe they were using the same language when actually they were not.

To regard incommensurability as a relation between existing linguistic structures or conceptual schemes, is to fall back on the notion of intranslatability. Since we cannot make sense of this notion, it makes no sense to think of two different natural languages as being incommensurable. The reason is that incommensurability is a diachronic relation, not a synchronic one; it is not a relation between structures, but a symptom of structural change. Such structural change can take the form of disintegration of a practice or a paradigm, as in scientific revolutions, or it can take the form of a merger of separate traditions, as when Evans-Pritchard went to live with the Azande.

When we are faced with a language other than our own, when we are attempting to *interpret* that language in terms of our own, we attempt this because we have not mastered the conventions that govern that language. And without the temporal viscosity of linguistic conventions, incommensurability can get no grip. If we do not understand a foreign tongue, this is because we are not perfect interpreters. It is never because the languages are somehow not commensurable. Incommensurability in discourse can only begin to occur once we *think* we have begun to agree on linguistic conventions, but in actuality remain confused as to what language we are using.

If we conceive of incommensurability as a certain kind of discourse that occurs as a result of changes in the conventional structure of the language, changes that affect the unity of that language, we may legitimately ask for an account of how those changes are generated, and how they are to be accommodated.

To the first of this questions, the answers will take the form of empirical, historical accounts, accounts that hermeneutically endeavour to show how and why particular changes in the use of terms or the application of standards occur. *The Structure of Scientific Revolutions* is precisely such an account. We can read Kuhn as showing the ways in which scientific innovations change the language of scientists. He also gives a theory of how those changes actually take place: they do not occur smoothly and gradually, with linguistic conventions imperceptibly altering over time. They occur in spurts and starts, disjointedly and locally, straining the language of a heretofore unified linguistic community past the breaking point. They cause, in other words, incommensurability in the discourse of scientists.

Other accounts in other fields of the same general phenomenon are both possible and desirable. Alasdair MacIntyre gives one in his book *After Virtue* (MacIntyre, 1981). He argues that the loss of the teleological conception of human life left the Enlightenment with an incoherent moral scheme, and that the various attempts at repairing this scheme resulted in different, and incommensurable, moral vocabularies. On my analysis, however, this incommensurability is not a particular relation among the different moral vocabularies, it is a characteristic of the discourse that results when we proceed *as if* we are using the same vocabulary, and so interpret others by applying linguistic conventions to which they are not party. MacIntyre's historical account of the failure of the Enlightenment project of justifying morality explains this incommensurability because it shows how a unified vocabulary lost its unity and broke up into fragments.

Similarly, a critique of the ideological co-option of language would also have to involve an account of incommensurability. It must be a critique that shows how a discrepancy between linguistic conventions and the meaning of what is said serves to disguise certain social facts. It should demonstrate how linguistic conventions have been manipulated, that is, how the production of meaning *via* a language has actually served to obscure linguistic understanding, and how this has served particular interests or social institutions.

These kinds of analysis are all accounts of the loss of the internal integrity of a structure. But, as suggested, incommensurability is likely to occur also when alien traditions meet. This is not, I must stress again, because alien traditions as such could turn out to be incommensurable, but because of the immensity of the task of penetrating the prejudices that cause us to misinterpret what is foreign, and so to mistake the language being spoken. This is why critical anthropology must also be a study of incommensurability.

The list of possible kinds of investigation into the phenomenon of incommensurability is likely to be endless. But all such accounts rely for their coherence on a semantics which can accommodate meaning-change without jeopardizing the possibility of linguistic understanding.

As suggested above, critical analyses of incommensurability must account not only for its genesis in the particular case, but also be informed by some theory of how to accommodate those structural changes in the body of conventions that disrupt the unity of a language. Any answer to this problem must arise out of our accounts of the causes of these changes. If incommensurable discourse is the result of an attempt to speak two (or more) languages at once, the result of a misapplication of linguistic conventions, then a concrete diagnosis is the first step towards a resolution. The realization that we are not speaking the same language is a condition of the possibility of renewed understanding. And if we can also provide an answer as to *why* we are not speaking the same language, translation might begin to improve.

Kuhn's work is an attempt to come up with just such an answer in the case of the evolution of that cluster of social practices we call science. There is a deep irony in the accusations of irrationalism voiced against him, since Kuhn's work provides just the sort of analysis that is needed if we are to overcome the breakdowns in communication characterized by incommensurability. Kuhn himself is not, perhaps, always entirely clear on this point, particularly in his phenomenological descriptions of incommensurability: he speaks, provocatively, of the switch from one paradigm to another as a conversion, and this is often understood as a conversion to a new way of seeing the world.[15] But on my account, what this conversion amounts to is learning and using a new language. When Kuhn says that, like the *Gestalt* switch, the conversion 'must occur all at once (though not necessarily in an instant) or not at all' (Kuhn, 1970, p. 150), he is not describing some mystical switch from one cognitive scheme to another. He is expressing the fact that we can only coherently speak one language at a time.

Notes

1 Some important responses to Kuhn are published in *Criticism and the Growth of Knowledge* (Lakatos and Musgrave, 1970). For a fairly representative slice of the philosophical debate about rationality, see the collections *Relativism* (Wilson, 1970), and *Rationality and Relativism* (Hollis and Lukes, 1982). However, as Bob Scholte points out in his excellent review of the latter, it 'is by-and-large a volume for and by rationalists' (Scholte, 1984, p. 962).

2 Popper, in 'Normal Science and its Dangers' (1970, pp. 51–8), takes Kuhn to be suggesting that paradigms 'are like mutually intranslatable languages' (p. 56), and this 'dangerous dogma' leads Kuhn straight to the relativistic 'Myth of the Framework', 'where no rational discussion is possible between frameworks' (p. 57). Shapere, too (1966 and 1971), argues that Kuhn's insistence that meanings change from one paradigm to another leaves us no way of comparing competing paradigms at all. Israel Scheffler makes the same charge of irrationalism in his book *Science and Subjectivity* (1967, see particularly ch.4), and again in 'Vision and Revolution; a Postscript on Kuhn' (1972), where he also slams Kuhn's use of the notion of a *gestalt* switch as a metaphor for what happens when one paradigm replaces another.

3 See also Winch's paper 'Understanding a Primitive Society' (1970). For a detailed analysis of the debates triggered by Kuhn and Winch and their common themes, see Richard Bernstein's *Beyond Objectivism and Relativism* (1983, particularly pp. 97–108).

4 See Rorty (1979, particularly ch. VII, sections 1 and 2), Bernstein (1983, Part Two) and Doppelt (1978). Doppelt's article, 'Kuhn's Epistemological Relativism: An Interpretation and Defence', is specifically addressed to the polemic of Scheffler and Shapere.

5 Feyerabend, like Kuhn, has been talking about incommensurability for three decades, but his most sustained analysis is found in chapter 17 of *Against Method* (Feyerabend, 1978). For an analysis of Feyerabend's position on incommensurability, see Rorty (1979, pp. 270–7) and Bernstein (1983, pp. 87–90).

6 The distinction between 'translation' and 'interpretation' as I employ these terms is not of great significance. All translation is also interpretation. I use 'translation' rather than 'interpretation' in the present context only to avoid a possible confusion with a use of 'interpretation' on which it contrasts with 'translation' (as in 'not translatable but interpretable...').

7 For an exposition and defence of the symmetry thesis (roughly, the idea that the truth of a belief is never sufficient as an explanation of why someone holds that belief), see Barnes and Bloor (1982). This article, 'Relativism, Rationalism and the Sociology of Knowledge', is a contribution to *Rationality and Relativism* (Hollis and Lukes, 1982). One of the foci of the debate in this book – whose other contributors without exception oppose Barnes and Bloor – is the question whether the translatability of different languages a priori precludes the possibility of relativism being true. See particularly William Newton-Smith's 'Relativism and the Possibility of Translation' (1982), where he claims that a consistent relativist would not even attempt to translate an unknown language.

8 This is also why the objection to the radical-interpretation conception of semantics brought out in Dummett's game analogy is not well taken: Dummett says that if we want to know what winning is, it is not enough to be told what counts as winning in a number of different games, 'for the rules of a game do not themselves explain, but take for granted, the significance of the classification which they impose upon final positions into winning ones and losing ones' (Dummett, 1973, p. 413). Similarly, he argues, if we want to know what truth is, it is not enough to be told what truth is in any number of different languages. (The analogy is developed further by Christopher Peacocke in his 'Truth Definitions and Actual Languages' (1976)). Davidson replies that the analogy is faulty, because there is nothing in a language which is like winning in a game in relevant respects (see *Inquiries*, p. 267). It seems to me, however, that the real point is just this: in terms of Dummett's analogy, what we want to

know is not what winning is, but how to play the game. Truth-theories for particular languages are not intended to illuminate a general concept of truth, but to construe the languages. Of course, they do this only if we know what it is for a particular theory to apply to a certain language. But as radical interpreters we do know this; a theory applies if it accommodates our observations.

9 Whorf's claim that there are cases when languages cannot be calibrated is one of the explicit targets of Davidson's attack on incommensurability. But a good case can be made for the view that Whorf's relativism (for which see Whorf, 1956) is not nearly as heady as Davidson and other philosophers have taken it to be. See, for example, Kay and Kempton (1984); in 'What is the Sapir—Whorf-Hypothesis?' Paul Kay and Willett Kempton suggest that we should regard the relativistic claims of anthropologists as part of the ongoing war against ethnocentrism waged by the practitioners of that discipline: 'Indeed', they say, 'outside of certain rarefied academic milieux, the early relativists' battle for a rational and unprejudiced view of our non-literate contemporaries is not yet won' (Kay and Kempton, 1984, p. 65). For a general and forceful statement of the view that philosophers' fear of the relativism they purport to detect in anthropology is unfounded, a result of a narrow epistemological concern with what he calls 'pasteurized knowledge', see Clifford Geertz's 'Distinguished Lecture: Anti Anti-Relativism', delivered to the American Anthropological Association (1984, pp. 263—78). See also Rorty's 'Pragmatism, Relativism, and Irrationalism' (1982) for a similar diagnosis.

10 Arguing that it is only in retrospect that crucial experiments emerge as crucial, Lakatos rejects justificationism, probabilism and naive falsificationism as 'theories of instant rationality — and instant learning . . .' These theories fail, according to Lakatos, because 'rationality works much slower than people think, and, even then, fallibly' (Lakatos, 1970, p. 74). But he makes what he takes to be a crucial distinction between Kuhn's position and his own account of competing research programmes: 'Kuhn's conceptual framework for dealing with continuity in science is socio-psychological: mine is normative . . . Where Kuhn sees "paradigms", I also see rational research programmes' (Lakatos, 1970, p. 177). For Lakatos, therefore, Kuhn's account, unlike Lakatos's own, fails to preserve the fundamental rationality of science: 'The new paradigm brings a totally new rationality. There are no super-paradigmatic standards. The change is a band-wagon effect. Thus in Kuhn's view scientific revolution is irrational, a matter for mob psychology' (Lakatos, 1970. p. 178).

11 Whether one interprets this as a sign of the richness of the paradigm concept or as a symptom of its vacuousness, depends on one's general commitments in the philosophy of science. Compare for instance Shapere's criticism in 'The Paradigm Concept' (1971) with Margaret Masterman's 'The Nature of a Paradigm' (1970). Masterman counts and documents 21 different senses of 'paradigm' as Kuhn uses it in *The Structure of Scientific Revolutions* (1970), yet, unlike Shapere, appears to find the concept a fruitful one.

12 The concept of a tradition is central to Gadamer's hermeneutics, as it is set forth in *Truth and Method* (1975). According to Gadamer:

> we stand always with tradition, and this is no objectifying process, i.e. we do not conceive of what tradition says as something other, something alien. It is always part of us, a model or exemplar, a recognition of ourselves which our later historical judgment would hardly see as a kind of knowledge, but as the simplest preservation of tradition. (Gadamer, 1975, p. 250)

> As Josef Bleicher puts it in his exposition of Gadamer: 'The interpreter is always embedded in a context of tradition which can … be regarded as the sharing of basic and supportive prejudices' (Bleicher, 1980, p. 110.) A prejudice — or prejudgement — in Gadamer's sense is not, of course, the same as an unwarranted or unjustifiable bias. Prejudices are, on the contrary, what constitute our pre-understanding, that in virtue of which we understand anything at all (cf. Gadamer, 1975, pp. 245–6). The epistemic values implicit in our comparative judgements about scientific theories can well be described as hermeneutic prejudices. The parallel between Kuhn and Gadamer is clear, and is emphasized by both Bernstein and Rorty.

13 As Gadamer stresses, the hermeneutics of *Truth and Method* is deeply rooted in Gadamer's reading of the *Nicomachean Ethics* (Aristotle).

14 Rorty's distinction between 'normal' and 'abnormal' discourse 'generalizes Kuhn's distinction between "normal" and "revolutionary" science' (Rorty, 1979, p. 320).

15 Kuhn himself contributed, for instance by the following infamous remark: 'In a sense that I am unable to explicate further, the proponents of competing paradigms practice their trades in different worlds' (Kuhn, 1970, p. 150).

10
Conclusion:
The Hermeneutics of Radical
Interpretation

Using Davidson's seminal work in semantics as my point of reference, I have, in the preceding chapters, developed a picture of linguistic communication as extensional, empirical, holistic and dynamic. It is extensional because the truth of its theorems is in the end the only necessary constraint on a theory of meaning for a language. It is empirical because determining the truth of its theorems is a matter of testing them against observable evidence. It is holistic because the meaning of a sentence is a function of its location in the semantic structure of a language as a totality. Finally, it is dynamic because linguistic understanding arises only through an ongoing process of theory construction and reconstruction.

This continuous construction and modification of truth-theories is radical interpretation. To determine the meaning of an utterance, then, is to subject it to radical interpretation by incorporating it in a theory of truth which places the utterance in a semantic pattern.

A semantics of interpretation contrasts with a semantics of languages. The fundamental premise of the latter is that what permits linguistic understanding is the mastery of a particular language. The question to be answered then becomes: What is it to master a language? And since this question appears to be answerable only by way of the concept of convention, a semantics of languages necessarily construes linguistic meaning as conventional.

In practice, communication succeeds because we master and make use of conventions. But conventions change over time. How does this affect communication? We can answer this question only if we have a concept of meaning to which conventions are not intrinsic. The radical-interpretation model provides us with just such a concept of meaning. Accordingly, we can distinguish the question of the nature of linguistic understanding from the question of what it is to speak a language. This distinction opens up the possibility of giving theoretical accounts of how structural changes in the body of conventions that is a language affect linguistic understanding.

Changes in linguistic conventions can be gradual, evolutionary, or they can occur abruptly, unevenly, in a way which disrupts the structural unity of a language. The linguistic manifestation of this disruption is incommensurability. Incommensurable discourse is a failure to interpret, a confusion about what language is being spoken. When conventions break down, or can no longer be taken for granted, linguistic meaning can be recovered only through radical interpretation.

Relying less on convention and more on observation in determining the meaning of what is said poses a hermeneutical task. As Gadamer says in 'Semantics and Hermeneutics': 'One of the fundamental structures of all speaking is that we are guided by preconceptions and anticipations in our talking in such a way that these continually remain hidden and that it takes a disruption in oneself of the intended meaning of what one is saying to become conscious of these prejudices as such' (Gadamer, 1976, p. 92). The idea of a radical interpreter is a limiting concept, an ideal figure whose interpretation of others is based entirely on observation. No actual speaker is able to achieve complete freedom from linguistic convention and still understand, or convey meaning. But even if it were possible to suspend linguistic convention entirely, the hermeneutical element of interpretation remains. For the act of observation itself is 'guided by preconceptions and anticipations' in the way Gadamer suggests. If radical interpretation comes easy, it is because interpreter and interpreted have similar ideas about what is worth talking about and what sorts of things are worth saying. When radical interpretation comes hard, it is a sign that there may be differences in fundamental values and interests. These differences make it difficult for the interpreter to know what to look for and where to look as she tries to pair off utterances with features (in the widest possible sense) of the world.

Awareness of a communication breakdown is not enough to overcome it. If interests and values diverge enough, mistranslation will be endemic. The result is, as suggested, incommensurability. To re-establish communication, it is necessary also to establish why mistranslation occurs. And this amounts to nothing less than an account of the ways in which our values and interests differ. It is the hermeneutic task of identifying these implicit prejudices of our understanding that is crystallized in the concept of radical interpretation.

The occurrence of incommensurability is actually an essential part of this hermeneutic process. For incommensurability is precisely a signal of a conflict of prejudgements and preconceptions. And it is only through conflict, through disruption, that it is possible 'to become conscious of these prejudices as such'. We remain unaware of our basic assumptions until faced with someone who does not share them.

The radical interpreter, free of convention, is completely fluid in her vacillation between taking an utterance as providing information about the world and taking it as conveying semantic information which requires a revision of her truth-theory. This enables her to make explicit the divergences in underlying assumptions that manifest themselves in mistranslation and lack of commensuration.

Radical interpretation is therefore both critical and reflexive. Guided methodologically by the attempt to maximize true theorems, the radical interpreter gains more by revising her own beliefs and assumptions than by attributing error to those she is trying to understand. What Gadamer says of the hermeneutically enlightened consciousness – opposing it to the unreflexive critique of prejudice – is also a description of the process of radical interpretation:

> [It establishes] a higher truth in that it draws itself into its own reflection. It's truth, namely, is that of translation. It is higher

because it allows the foreign to become one's own, not by destroying it critically or reproducing it uncritically, but by explicating it within one's own horizons with one's own concepts and thus giving it new validity. (Gadamer, 1976, p. 94)

In the dialectical movement of reflexive, critical understanding, incommensurability is what provides the opportunity for self-transcendence, or, in Gadamer's terms, the fusion of horizons. A semantics of interpretation is indispensable to all critical theory because it permits us, as I have shown, to diagnose and locate incommensurability as a linguistic phenomenon:

By making such observations semantic analysis is able, in a manner of speaking, to read the differences in times and the course of history. In particular, it has a vantage point from which to make the intrusion of one structural totality into another total structure recognizable. Its descriptive precision points up the incoherence that results when a realm of words is carried over into new contexts — and such incongruity often indicates that something truly new has been discovered. (Gadamer, 1976, pp. 84–5)

Bibliography

Appiah, A. (1986), *For Truth in Semantics*, Blackwell.

Aristotle, *The Nicomachean Ethics*, translated by David Ross, Oxford University Press, first published in 1925.

Barnes, B. and Bloor, D. (1982), 'Relativism, Rationalism and the Sociology of Knowledge', In M. Hollis and S. Lukes (eds), *Rationality and Relativism*, Blackwell, 21–47.

Bernstein, R. (1983), *Beyond Objectivism and Relativism*, University of Pennsylvania Press.

Bilgrami A. (1986), 'Meaning, Holism and Use'. In E. LePore (ed.), *Truth and Interpretation*, Blackwell, 101–22.

Bleicher, J. (1980), *Contemporary Hermeneutics*, Routledge and Kegan Paul.

Carloye, J. (1985), 'Normal Science and the Extension of Theories'. *British Journal for the Philosophy of Science*, 36, 241–56.

Davidson, D. (1974), 'Replies to David Lewis and W. V. Quine'. *Synthese*, 27, 345–9.

—— (1980a), *Essays on Actions and Events*, Clarendon Press.

—— (1980b), 'Toward a Unified Theory of Meaning and Action'. *Grazer Philosophische Studien*, 2, 1–12.

—— (1984), *Inquiries into Truth and Interpretation*, Clarendon Press.

—— (1986a), 'A Nice Derangement of Epitaphs'. In E. LePore (ed.), *Truth and Interpretation*, Blackwell, 433–46.

—— (1986b), 'A Coherence Theory of Truth and Knowledge'. In E. LePore (ed.), *Truth and Interpretation*, Blackwell, 307–19.

—— (1986c) 'Empirical Content'. In E. LePore (ed.), *Truth and Interpretation*, Blackwell, 320–32.

—— (1988), 'Meaning, Truth and Evidence'. Delivered at the Quine Conference, St. Louis, April (ms).

Descartes, R. (1639), 'Letter to Mersenne'. In A. Kenny (ed.) Philosophical Letters of René Descartes, Clarendon Press.

Devitt, M. (1981), *Designation*, Columbia University Press.

—— (1985), *Realism and Truth*, Blackwell.

Donnellan, K. (1962), 'Necessity and Criteria'. *Journal of Philosophy*, LIX, 647—58.

—— (1966), 'Reference and Definite Descriptions'. *Philosophical Review*, LXXV, 281—304.

—— (1972), 'Proper Names and Identifying Descriptions'. In D. Davidson and G. Harman (eds), *Semantics of Natural Language*, D. Reidel Publishing Company, 356—79.

Doppelt, G. (1978), 'Kuhn's Epistemological Relativism: An Interpretation and Defence'. *Inquiry*, 21, 33—86.

Dummett, M. A. E. (1973), *Frege: Philosophy of Language*, Duckworth.

—— (1975), 'What is a Theory of Meaning?'. In S. Guttenplan (ed.) *Mind and Language*, Clarendon Press, 97—138.

—— (1976), 'What is a Theory of Meaning? (II)', In G. Evans and J. McDowell (eds) *Truth and Meaning*, Clarendon Press, 67—137.

—— (1978), 'The Significance of Quine's Indeterminacy Thesis'. In *Truth and Other Enigmas*, Harvard University Press, pp. 375—419.

—— (1986) 'Comments on Davidson and Hacking'. In E. LePore (ed.), *Truth and Interpretation*, Blackwell, 459—76.

Evans, G. and McDowell, J. (eds.) (1976), *Truth and Meaning*, Clarendon Press.

Feyerabend, P. (1978), *Against Method*, Verso.

Field, H. (1972), 'Tarski's Theory of Truth'. *Journal of Philosophy*, 69, 347—75.

—— (1975), 'Conventionalism and Instrumentalism in Semantics'. *Nous*, 9, 375—405.

—— (1978), 'Mental Representation'. *Erkenntnis*, 13.

Fodor, J. (1975), *The Language of Thought*, Thomas Y. Crowell.

—— (1987), *Psychosemantics*, M.I.T. Press.

Foster, J. A. (1976), 'Meaning and Truth Theory'. In G. Evans and J. McDowell, *Truth and Meaning*, Clarendon Press, 1—32.

Frege, G. (1962), 'On Sense and Reference'. In M. Black and P. T. Geach (eds), *Philosophical Writings*, Oxford.

Gadamer, H.-G. (1975), *Truth and Method*, Sheed and Ward. This translation is based on the 2nd edn (1965) of *Warheit und Methode*, the 1st edn of which was published in 1960 by J. C. B. Mohr (Paul Siebech), Tubingen.

—— (1976), 'Semantics and Hermeneutics'. In *Philosophical Hermeneutics*, University of California Press.

Geertz, C. (1984), 'Distinguished Lecture: Anti Anti-Relativism'. *American Anthropologist*, 86, 263−78.

Hacking, I. (1975), *Why Does Language Matter to Philosophy?*, Cambridge University Press.

—— (1984), 'On the Frontier', a review of Davidson (1982). *New York Review of Books*, 20 Dec.

—— (1986), 'The Parody of Conversation'. In E LePore (ed.), *Truth and Interpretation*, Blackwell, 447−58.

Hesse, M. (1980), *Revolutions and Reconstructions in the Philosophy of Science*, Indiana University Press.

Hofstadter, D. and Dennett, D. C. (eds) (1982), *The Mind's I*, Bantam Books.

Hollis, M. and Lukes, S. (eds) (1982), *Rationality and Relativism*, Blackwell.

Katz, J. J. (1979), 'The Neoclassical Theory of Reference'. In P. A. French, T. E. Uehling Jr. and H. K. Weltstein (eds), *Contemporary Perspectives in the Philosophy of Language*, University of Minnesota Press, 103−24.

—— (1986), 'Why Intensionalists Ought Not Be Fregeans'. In E. LePore *Truth and Interpretation*, Blackwell, 59−91.

Kay, P. and Kempton, W. (1984), 'What is the Sapir−Whorf-Hypothesis?' *American Anthropologist*, 86, 65−79.

Kripke, S. (1972), 'Naming and Necessity' In D. Davidson and G. Harman (eds), *Semantics of Natural Language*, D. Reidel Publishing Company, 253−355.

Kuhn, T. S. (1970), *The Structure of Scientific Revolutions*, 2nd edn, enlarged, The University of Chicago Press.

Lakatos, I. (1970), 'Falsification and the Methodology of Scientific Research Programmes'. In I. Lakatos and A. Musgrave (eds), *Criticism and the Growth of Knowledge*, Cambridge University Press, 91−195.

Lakatos, I. and Musgrave, A. (eds) (1970), *Criticism and the Growth of Knowledge*, Cambridge University Press.

Lewis, D. (1969), *Convention: A Philosophical Study*, Harvard University Press.

—— (1974), 'Radical Interpretation'. *Synthese*, 27, 331−44.

—— (1975), 'Languages and Language'. In K. Gunderson (ed.) *Language, Mind, and Knowledge*, (Minnesota Studies in the Philosophy of Science, vol. VII), University of Minnesota Press, 3−35.

Loar, B. (1976), 'Two Theories of Meaning'. In G. Evans and J. McDowell (eds), *Truth and Meaning*, Clarendon Press, 138−61.

Lukes, S. (1982), 'Relativism in its Place'. In M. Hollis and S. Lukes (eds), *Rationality and Relativism*, Blackwell, 261−305.

MacIntyre, A. (1981), *After Virtue*, University of Notre Dame Press.

A. Masterman, M. (1970), 'The Nature of a Paradigm'. In I. Lakatos and A. Musgrave (eds) *Criticism and the Growth of Knowledge*, Cambridge University Press, 59–89.

Mates, B. (1952), 'Synonymity'. In L. Linsky (ed.), *Semantics and the Philosophy of Language*, Urbana, 111–38.

Newton-Smith, W. (1982), 'Relativism and the Possibility of Translation'. In M. Hollis and S. Lukes (eds) *Rationality and Relativism*, Blackwell, 106–22.

Peacocke, C. (1976) 'Truth Definitions and Actual Languages'. In G. Evans and J. MacDowell (eds) *Truth and Meaning*, Clarendon Press, 162–88.

Popper, K. (1970) 'Normal Science and its Dangers'. In I. Lakatos and A. Musgrave (eds), *Criticism and the Growth of Knowledge*, Cambridge University Press, 51–58.

Putnam, H. (1962), 'It Ain't Necessarily so'. *Journal of Philosophy*, LIX, 658–71.

—— (1975), 'The Meaning of "Meaning"'. In *Mind, Language, and Reality* (Philosophical Papers, vol. 1), Cambridge University Press.

—— (1981), *Reason, Truth and History*, Cambridge University Press.

Quine, W. V. (1960), *Word and Object*, M.I.T. Press.

—— (1961), 'Two Dogmas of Empiricism'. In *From a Logical Point of View*, 2nd edn, revised, Harvard University Press.

—— (1969a), 'Ontological Relativity'. In *Ontological Relativity and Other Essays*, Columbia University Press, 26–68.

—— (1969b), 'Epistemology Naturalized'. In *Ontological Relativity and Other Essays*, Columbia University Press, 69–90.

—— (1969c), 'Speaking of Objects'. In *Ontological Relativity and Other Essays*, Columbia University Press.

—— (1981a), 'Empirical Content'. In *Theories and Things*, Harvard University Press, 24–30.

—— (1981b), 'On the Very Idea of a Third Dogma'. In *Theories and Things*, Harvard University Press 38–42.

—— (1981c), 'Use and its Place in Meaning'. In *Theories and Things*, Harvard University Press, 43–54.

Rorty, R. (1979), *Philosophy and the Mirror of Nature*, Princeton University Press.

—— (1982), 'Pragmatism, Relativism, and Irrationalism'. In *Consequences of Pragmatism*, University of Minnesota Press.

—— (1986), 'Pragmatism, Davidson and Truth'. In E. LePore (ed.), *Truth and Interpretation*, Blackwell, 333–55.

Scheffler, I. (1967), *Science and Subjectivity*, Dobbs-Merrill Company.

—— (1972), 'Vision and Revolution; a Postscript on Kuhn'. *Philosophy of Science*, 39, 366—74.

Scholte, B. (1984), 'Reason and Culture: The Universal and the Particular Revisited'. *American Anthropologist*, 86, 960—5.

Shapere, D. (1966), 'Meaning and Scientific Change'. In R. Colodny (ed.), *Mind and Cosmos: Essays in Contemporary Science and Philosophy*, University of Pittsburgh Press, 41—85.

—— (1971), 'The Paradigm Concept'. *Science*, 172, 706—9.

Stampe, D. W. (1979), 'Towards a Causal Theory of Linguistic Representation'. In P. A. French, T. E. Uehling Jr. and H. K. Wettstein (eds), *Contemporary Perspectives in the Philosophy of Language*, University of Minnesota Press, 81—102.

Tarski, A. (1956), 'The Concept of Truth in Formalized Languages'. In *Logic, Semantics, Metamathematics* (papers from 1923 to 1938), Clarendon Press, 152—278.

Vermazen B. (1986), 'Testing Theories of Interpretation'. In E. LePore (ed.) *Truth and Interpretation*, Blackwell, 235—44.

Wallace, J. (1986), 'Translation Theories and the Decipherment of Linear B'. In E. LePore (ed.) *Truth and Interpretation*, Blackwell, 211—34.

Wettstein, H. K. (1984), 'How to Bridge the Gap Between Meaning and Reference'. *Synthese*, 58, 163—84.

Whorf, B. L. (1956), *Language, Thought and Reality*, M.I.T. Press.

Wilson, B. (ed.) (1970), *Relativism*, Blackwell.

Winch, P. (1958), *The Idea of a Social Science and its Relation to Philosophy*, Routledge and Kegan Paul.

—— (1970), 'Understanding a Primitive Society'. In B. Wilson (ed.) *Relativism*, Blackwell, 78—111.

Wittgenstein, L. (1958), *Philosophical Investigations*, 2nd edn, Blackwell.

Index

DATE DUE

JUN 08 1990		
JUN 03 RECD		
SEP 0		
MAY 09 RECD		